# POST-MORTEM
# JOURNAL

# Post-Mortem Journal

*Communications from T. E. Lawrence*

JANE SHERWOOD

THE C.W. DANIEL COMPANY LIMITED
SAFFRON WALDEN

First published in Great Britain
by Neville Spearman Limited

This edition published by
The C.W. Daniel Company Limited
1 Church Path, Saffron Walden
Essex, CB10 1JP, England
1991

ISBN 0 85207 253 8

*Produced in Great Britain by*
*Ennisfield Print & Design, London*

# Post-Mortem Journal

# Contents

Introduction                                           9
1   An End and a Beginning                            15
2   Early Experiences and Experiments                 25
3   Sowing and Reaping                                40
4   Exploring                                         46
5   Adventures in the World of Thought                60
6   The University: A Transition                      70
7   Purgation                                         83
8   Friends and Associates                           102
9   Our World and its People                         114
10  The New Vision                                   124

# Introduction

THIS BOOK REPRESENTS the last phase in a long series of communications which began in 1938. Automatic writing has been for me a means of acquiring information in the life-long search for light on the puzzling problems of our existence. For it is only when we close our eyes to the mystery that surrounds our life that these problems can be ignored. Let an hour of solitude, a mood of introspection seize us and we find ourselves out on that desolate shore Keats knew when he wrote:

> Then on the shores of this wide world I
> stand and think
> Till love and fame to nothingness do shrink.

Our little islands of existence are indeed surrounded by an ocean of mystery – an ocean that religion offers to sound, that philosophy tries to chart, that science has decided to ignore – but upon which we each must eventually launch our lonely vessel.

In the early days of my work three communicators used my pen and of these 'Scott' was one. He helped in building up a picture of after-death conditions and relating them to our life here and now. Scott's contributions were always recognisable for their vivid and tonic qualities and sometimes for the unconscious arrogance with which they were presented. His sense of fun often lit up serious interchanges of thought and made working with him a delight. I am grateful for this long association with a keen and unorthodox mind. Since in 1959 we finished this intimate account of his experiences, which at his own suggestion is called *Post-Mortem Journal* he has ceased to communicate. The reason may be found in the nature of the after-death conditions he describes and in his own development to a stage where communication becomes more difficult, or it may be that the slowing down of his swifter processes to synchronise with our sluggish rate of thought has now become intolerable. It was never easy for him; I retain an impish thought image he once passed to me of himself running frantically in circles around me and even turning somersaults in his impatience at my slowness. Whatever his reason, this seems to be all I shall be able to pass on of his continuing life and thought.

The method of working by taking automatic writing in full consciousness is open to many objections. It can be dismissed as a mere outpouring from the unconscious mind and indeed, where it degenerates into rambling incoherences and imitative fantasies this interpretation seems likely to be true. But we are a long way yet from understanding the process and may well suspend judgement until we know more about the human psyche and its many ways of acquiring knowledge. May it not be that in addition to the Freudian unconscious – a kind of scrapheap of undesirable memories and impulses, there may also be a part of the mind, normally inaccessible to consciousness it is true, but which is a channel through which spiritual knowledge filters through into consciousness? Is it not conceivable that this higher part of the unconscious mind, when in a state of activation, may be used by discarnate intelligence to convey meaningful information? Until we have more understanding of the powers and scope of the human mind our only criterion is the quality of the communications themselves and in our present state of ignorance this is the only way in which the work can be judged.

The riddle of 'Scott's' identity is not difficult to guess. He is Colonel T. E. Lawrence. He first wrote for me in 1938 and from the beginning he used his own name. But as soon as any question of publication arose he demanded of me a promise to respect his anonymity. This promise I gave. I found in him always an ambivalent attitude towards his public image. It undoubtedly had a strong attraction for him and any reference to his name in the press produced a strong agitation which, reflected as it had to be upon my own mind often shook me badly. Had it been straightforward joy or even unmixed annoyance it would have been easier to bear. In process of time this reaction decreased in power and almost disappeared as though he had at last become indifferent to his fame. The change no doubt marked his progress. In *Post-Mortem Journal* he has taken very little trouble to conceal his identity and I think we may conclude that it is no longer a matter of concern to him.

In this account of his life and conditions, 'Scott' uses terms which were employed by the group when he shared in the writing of previous books*. They are not ideal terms and I think we all used them with reluctance. Such words as 'astral' for instance, used to describe not only planes of being but also the kind of body which replaces the physical at death, are convenient but suspect. By derivation, 'astral, of the stars' is irrelevant and by common use it is tainted by association with the less reputable practices of the seance room. But some term must be used and it is confusing to the reader if he has to become used to a set of unfamiliar and arbitrarily invented terms. So the traditional ones have been retained as the lesser of two evils.

As to the account of 'Scott's' actual experiences, I suspect that they are sometimes expressed in more concrete terms than was intended. Their translation into our words has been done, after all, through a mind conditioned only to earth experience. Our language was never intended to convey the shades and subtleties of other worldly truth with exactitude and the writer has been only too aware of the meanings which so often 'broke through language and escaped'. If what I have written falls short of the truth, the reader may know that the truth is something greater. I cannot express the sense of frustration and despair with which I have realised my own inadequacy.

At this point the reliability of the medium becomes important. Inadequacy I admit; but I can and do vouch for my own honesty. What I have received is here set down and the reader must judge of its probability for himself.

JANE  SHERWOOD

* *The Psychic Bridge* and *The Country Beyond*.

# Chapter 1

⧉⧉

## AN END AND A BEGINNING

A SHATTERING BLOW, darkness rent with interludes of throbbing agony and finally merciful cessation of pain; nothingness.

Out of the void came first a mere point of self-awareness, lost and found again and spreading gradually into an indefinite impression of being; a sensation of neither darkness nor light, an uneasy greyness filled with growing apprehension. Soon I should need to drag myself out of this numbing stupor, to find out where I was and what was happening in this waste of greyness. But having flickered, consciousness went out again and I slept.

There came a time when I could no longer drowse my fears away. The sense of identity grew stronger and with it came a tumult of emotions and hurried, anxious thoughts. Unwillingly I had to awake to a formless world of which I seemed the only inhabitant. Yet I thought I heard voices but could distinguish no words; I felt the shadows palpitate with movement and could see no one. I was aware, too, of waves of sorrow washing up around me and trying to drown my feeble consciousness. Becoming aware of my body I found myself on my feet, surprised to find movement so light and easy, but I was afraid to venture far in any direction because of the shadowy obstacles I sensed around. I fumbled in the dimness, seeking a way out of the grief that enveloped me. Where was I? Even if I had become blind and deaf surely there must be someone around to help me? I tried calling, but there was no response. What had happened?

At first my mind was entirely occupied with my predicament and the past did not concern me, but as I wandered now one, now another vision flashed across my mental retina. A ribbon of road, boys on bicycles, my cottage, and soon these discrete memories began to coalesce into a continuous series of past experiences. Before long I was racing back along the years faster and faster, helpless to stay the record and obliged to feel as well as to remember as my past unrolled back to the earliest childhood memories. I had come to a stand while this disquieting survey held me and as it checked at the unconsciousness of the infant my own consciousness flickered out. At the very moment of oblivion I gasped with relief and just had time to think: this is really the end.

It was not. After a long or short interval – how should I know? – I came to myself again, mildly surprised because I had not expected existence to continue and certainly had as yet no reason to welcome it. The dimness had lifted a little and a world of vague outlines was developing out of the mist; meadows, I thought, hedges and trees. Perhaps the blurred outlines in the distance were houses? A town perhaps, people. I did not want to meet people. For the first time I realised that I was naked but apart from this embarrassment I shrank from my kind and even preferred the empty solitude. But in thinking of the town and what it might hold I found myself drifting towards it and thus got my first indication of the way movement here is affected by thought. I obstinately resisted this drift towards the town and turned away to explore the open country.

All this while the light had been strengthening and the greyness lifting. Soon the dreary place could be distinguished as a gloomy November dusk and I could move freely without the fear of stumbling into shadows and finding they were substance. I came upon a convenient bank and rested. I was not conscious of cold and forgot my nakedness. As I sat there it became possible to think more clearly and to take stock of my position. All my known and familiar world was gone and if this was a nightmare I still had to abide the awakening. The startling impression that this was death became insistent, but if I had to accept that idea what became of my conviction that death ended it all? For I was certainly alive, if you could call it living, and it even appeared that my surroundings were taking on more substance and I myself more vitality. So any expectation that this was just a particularly persistent nightmare became unlikely. I felt my body; firm flesh. How odd! I tried to speak but only a throttled ghost of a sound came forth. I arose and walked and realised afresh how light and resilient my limbs felt. So back to my bank to think afresh.

Suppose for the sake of argument that this was death; what kind of world was this? I thought with a pang of 'Sheol', place of the Shade. It was that, all right. Had Charon already rowed me over the dark river and was this the accursed Hades? If so, the Greeks had been right after all, as they nearly always were. My thought seemed as bound by shadows as my surroundings. All life and living was reduced to a monochrome. No sound, no movement, no light, no joy: only a dreary acquiescence in this half-light, half-living. A grievous lassitude invaded me. Existence, endurance; endurance, existence. How much better to have flickered out for good!

How long this weary experience lasted I cannot guess. Weeks? Months? I walked about. I sat. I experimented with my new powers of motion. I even began to make recognisable sounds and either I had got used to my conditions or my sight was sharpening for my vision was clearing. Moreover, the cloud of depression and despair had begun to lift from my mind and a desire for action began to stir. But what to do in this desert?

My thought turned towards the town I had seen. If

I had to come to terms with this existence I must first find out more about its conditions. In my wanderings I had long ago lost sight of the blur on the horizon and I had no idea of its direction. But as though the wish had the power to direct me, my steps were drawn in the right way and before long I saw the roofs and chimneys of a small town ahead. The scene as I approached it was so like any town I might have visited on earth that the ever-present thought that this was not earth but the country of the dead began to leave me. So ordinary, so drearily earth-like were the outskirts of the hamlet; rows of small, mean houses, shops, even the usual depressing chapel I passed and so went on towards the centre which might have belonged to any English market town. There were people going about their business. They were not prepossessing either in appearance or manners. They took no particular notice of my unclothed condition, but finding a shop where ready-made garments were on show I went in, forgetting for the moment that I lacked the wherewithal to pay. The man behind the counter grinned uncivilly but to my surprise simply pointed to his stock and said 'help yourself'. I thought it better to comply without comment; in any case, what could I say? I picked out some serviceable light garments and put them on, thanked him and departed. He appeared to accept this as normal behaviour so I went on my way marvelling.

I decided to accost someone and ask for information but the passing faces had in them no signs of friendliness so I wandered on oppressed by my loneliness. True, I could now hear clearly, I could speak and sight was becoming clearer. But whether the fault of my vision or a characteristic of the locality, the same dingy murk prevailed and the place and the people were all of a piece; hard-featured women with shrill, harsh voices and men whose faces were marked by brutality and meanness came from the houses and mingled uneasily in the streets.

Near panic began to mount in me and the more my loneliness and fear increased the more menacing seemed my surroundings. My only thought now was to get clear of the place and no sooner was the decision formed than my feet drew me swiftly back to the outskirts and away from the gloomy place. I did not stop until I had put a considerable distance between myself and the last of the houses; then I paused and found a convenient resting place. I felt again the need to understand what was happening to me and if possible discover how to turn these queer conditions to a useful end.

I had stumbled upon at least one principle which might have valuable consequences. My own desire could lead me towards its fulfilment if I knew clearly what I wanted. I certainly did not desire any further acquaintance with the place and people I had just left but I still had to discover whether any better were to be found. Sitting there and trying to decide on my next move I began to get a peculiar feeling as of a presence at my side, though, turning quickly, I saw no one. I knew it to be a friendly presence at least, and soon I made out words sounding close to my ear.

'You need help?' it asked.

'I do indeed,' I replied. 'Why cannot I see you?'

My new friend replied, 'You have got yourself into a very unhappy region and as I can see that you do not belong here I should like to help. Who are you?'

I gave him my name and was relieved to find that it told him nothing. At least I could leave behind my tiresome notoriety. He went on: 'You must have been in a wretched state of mind before you came here and that accounts for waking in this part of the world. We must get you into a happier condition before we can help you much.'

As he spoke I saw that a light had diffused itself around us and I smiled with pleasure at the first brightness I had seen in this dreary Hades.

'Come, that is better already,' he said, and I felt warmth and reassurance stealing over me as he spoke.

'Now, if you are able, come with me,' he said, and although I thought this might not be so easy since as yet I could not see him my feet were led and I went, keeping always near to the light and warmth of his presence.

He took me quietly over an ever-brightening landscape and explained as we went that my newly developing senses had to be given time to adjust to their new world and that this new world would only hold for me what I was capable of seeing in it.

'So the gloomy town was only a reflection of my state; or is it an actual place?' I asked.

'Unfortunately it is actual enough for those who

want nothing better. They have not yet developed the power to live in any other way,' he replied. 'They make their own atmosphere by the emanations of their own rather horrid emotions and I see that you found it uncongenial enough to get free of it quickly. They are not very pleasant folk there and they might soon have sensed your difference and resented it and then there might have been trouble. Not that they could have injured you in the physical way you are thinking of, but a lot of undesirable emotions would have been let loose and you would have suffered from these. To encounter active ill-will is for us a painful experience, but all this will become easier to understand when you know more about this world.'

I explained that I had already discovered that a strong desire could be used as a directing agent and that my fear and loathing of the place had helped me to get away from it.

'I was trying to think how to use this power to find a more congenial place and people, if such exist,' I said. 'The trouble was that I could not know that there was anything else and the thought of an endless continuance in those conditions was appalling. Then I became aware that I was not alone and you can imagine my gratitude for your help. May I know who you are?'

'My name is Mitchell,' he said. 'It won't convey anything to you but I work with newcomers and was here when you came into view.'

I felt suddenly constrained and diffident and the change must have been obvious to him for he said:

'Don't do that, for God's sake, or I can't stay. You have to learn that your feelings create an atmosphere about you that alters your relationship to those you meet.'

I shrank away and his light dimmed. In alarm I called to him and he heard me and returned.

'I think I had better find someone you have known to help you,' he said, but I was ashamed and begged him to stay. So again we went on together and he explained to me that my present body, being of such a light, responsive kind, would express in its colour and emanations every emotion I felt so that not the slightest change of mood could be hidden.

'I begin to understand then, the unstable state of my feelings,' I said. 'I hope you will forgive me. I am raw and prickly all over and it affects me as though physically. I do not know how to adjust to your kindness nor to control the surges of emotion. You must think me a most ungrateful cuss,' I said.

'No,' he said. 'I understand the difficulty too well. At first one is all over the place. But the less you worry about other people's reactions to you the better; the more happy and at your ease you can feel the easier it will be for you and for us.'

'This is going to be difficult,' I said. 'I have less control of my feelings than I thought possible; in fact, they hardly answer to control at all. Great waves of emotion take me off my balance. How long will it be before I can reach a state of equilibrium?'

'I shall take you, with your permission, to a kind of sanatorium where I work,' he said. 'There they will go on helping you and giving you the right conditions for health.'

'All this is very intriguing, if uncomfortable,' I said. 'It isn't going to be the effortless sort of heaven one would have expected if one hadn't been so stupid as to expect nothing at all.'

'Is that what you thought?' Mitchell asked. 'It seems very stupid now, as you say. But it helps to explain your difficulties before I found you.'

Thinking of this place to which I was being taken I felt an instant's reluctance and again his warning voice reminded me that it would affect him.

'Trust me,' he said, 'and you will not regret it.'

My vision had been strengthening as we went and I could now see my guide. He was tall and dark with deep-set, kindly eyes. Raying out from him light in warm tones enveloped and comforted me too. I decided to trust to his leadership and advice, for confidence in my own powers had gone. I found myself in a strange world, moved by urgent emotions over which I had little control. I swayed and trembled in this unknown world defenceless and afraid.

# Chapter 2

EARLY EXPERIENCES AND EXPERIMENTS

UP TO THE present my experiences have been dreamlike – almost nightmarish at times. There has been an
unreal quality in my surroundings, and in myself a
feeling of shadowy and unsubstantial being. I still miss
the weight of my earth body, I suppose, although I
should be sorry now to have to drag it about. Yet in
spite of my lightness and weightlessness I am moved
by powerful pangs of emotion which I find almost impossible to control. In a peculiar way these feelings are
more exterior to experiences; I myself, the real 'I' seem
to have retreated further inside and these emotions,
although they are mine and very powerful, are not felt
as the essential inward things they were on earth. This
new body is very responsive to incoming impressions;

25

too much so for my present comfort. It is like driving
a very fast and powerful car when one has only been
used to a slow second-hand one. I dislike the insecurity
and uncertainty this gives me although I cannot help
being exhilarated by the potential power at my dis-
posal. More than all, I dislike the idea that these waves
of emotion, whether they are desirable or not, are
apparent to everyone I meet.

Speaking of these impressions to Mitchell he explained to me that my present body, solid as it seems,
is now really composed of a kind of matter which on
earth I thought of as 'emotion'. This 'feeling stuff' is
now exterior to the real me and has no physical drag
to slow down its activity. Hence the frightening release
of emotional energy and the impossibility of masking
it. I now have to practise, not to mask my feelings, because this is no longer possible, but to control them
and to work at getting rid of the undesirable ones
altogether. He warned me that it would be hard work
at first, but that with help I should soon become
adjusted.

This has reduced me to silence and despair again. I
know only too well the volcano of emotion I have
always had to suppress and now suppression will not
avail me. As though he had read my thought, Mitchell
said: 'Don't despair. Millions of less gifted people
have managed it so I am sure it can be done.'

Whether as a result of realising the size of the job
ahead of me or not, I don't know, but I was over-
taken then by a great weariness. Mitchell advised me
to give in to it and sleep. Unconsciousness took me

suddenly and completely and I knew nothing more for some time. When I awoke we continued on our journey and I finally found myself inside a pleasant building and in a bright open room where other men were lounging and talking among themselves. Mitchell had disappeared but a young looking man came up to me and greeted me. We compared our experiences and I found that he too was a newcomer. Unfortunately he recognised me but my dismay was so obvious that he agreed to keep his counsel. I wanted time to find out more about this life and about myself and my new make-up before I had to take up the burden of being myself again. I had to learn to control and use a powerful machine that was strange to me and might easily get out of hand. So I begged to be left alone for awhile.

I have decided to make a record of my experiences here. They have been so odd and bizarre up to the present and the future promises to be even more strange and exciting. So from time to time I shall note down my reflections on this strange world.

I have been given a small room full of lovely colours and light and here I can be assured of solitude. I feel that another talk with Mitchell would help me. He has an experienced confidence which gives me strength and encouragement. Forgetting what a strong desire can do I was wishing for his presence when my feet carried me swiftly out of my room, down several corridors and into a quiet room where my friend sat writing. He half turned from his desk as though expecting me and he laughed when he saw my surprise.

'You must not be so imperious in your wishes if you do not want to be rapidly whirling about all the time,' he said.

I enjoyed my first laugh at my own expense and was delighted at the scintillating colours our mirth set going. The feeling of unreality is, I find, wearing off, and Mitchell in particular is taking on the substantial aspect of actuality. We settled down for a long talk in the course of which he told me plainly that in order to be able to help me he would have to probe into my past. I do realise now that accustomed reticences are no longer possible and that in this queer life one's only chance of prospering is to accept what one is and try to do something with it. This conclusion brings a refreshing easing of tension and a sense of release.

Probe he did and he soon had the whole story of ambition, mixed motives, success and its dead-sea fruits. Yet as I told the story I was well aware that he was reading behind my words to the emotions behind them and seeing both more and less than I had the courage to say. I should bitterly have resented such an intrusion into my personal life in the old days but I am learning fast that I can no longer hide inconvenient aspects of my personality and that if I let myself resent their discovery I make an atmosphere which drives everyone away. Luckily Mitchell had great delicacy and adopted such an objective attitude that I could just bear his scrutiny with equanimity.

Then he startled me.

'I am worried about the repressions you have practised and I don't think we can get a proper balance
until you have let go on them,' he said.

'You mean – ?' I asked.

'You have lived a monk-like existence and my
advice to you is to go and experiment with all the experiences you missed on earth. Go on a proper spree.
Don't tell yourself that you are too fastidious and don't
want to. Deep down you both want to and need to. Unless you can release some of the forbidden desires the
amount of stored and dangerous emotion will constantly overset your equilibrium and keep you in a
state of turmoil. Hence my advice to you to open the
safety valves. There are many things to make clear to
you which will make such a course less distasteful. My
dear fellow, I am not counselling irresponsibility but at
present you are such a dangerous volcano of eruptive
forces that you will not be able to make progress here.
If I am to get you right for this plane you must be
content to go lower for awhile and compensate by
some really riotous living for all you have chosen to
miss.'

This diagnosis was a shock and has thrown me into
a worse state of turmoil than ever. For awhile I sat
silent and I suppose my agitation was too strong, for
when I looked up again my friend had gone. I have to
get used to these sudden comings and goings but on
this occasion I was glad to be alone.

I have never been more at a loss. Suppose I agree
to do my best to do my worst, as it were; how to set
about it? I have wandered back to my own room to

ponder Mitchell's advice. My earthly standards apparently will not do here; all is topsy-turvy. Here is a responsible and serious doctor telling me quite calmly to go to the devil and I, a monk-like solitary am seriously contemplating taking his advice. I can begin to understand too that the advice is good. The reserve of emotional power which has driven me so hard in life; the restless activity, the impatience, the craving for speed – this overload of power is now too strong for its frailer body. Some blood-letting is indicated. But again, how to set about it?

I had left the building as these thoughts were passing and now have reached a hilltop from which a wide area of glowing and beautiful country can be seen. I shall rest here and consider my situation. It is exciting and yet rather alarming to know that I have only to desire and my feet will be led in the right direction. Let me try to bring my wishes into focus. I think of women I have known; tall, short, fair and dark. I try to picture the not-impossible-she, but my wishes have no power. The whole idea is too novel and I cannot come to grips with it. The range of choice is too wide and indefinite. Self-defeated, I can wish for none of them. This is a worse frustration than ever. Does it mean that I am so self-divided as to be incapable of action at all, emotionally impotent, in fact? Luckily I am alone, for at this thought hot resentment and shame are flaring up and the display of fiery, ugly colouring that is coming from me is not pleasant. I have let it subside and now have tried again. A girl I once knew well; shall I seek her out? Perhaps she has already formed ties, perhaps – and no, I cannot contemplate it. The situation is impossible and I decide that I need help and a companion in this adventure. So back to the home.


I do not propose to detail all my hesitations and doubts nor my struggle with diffidence and life-long inhibitions. The monk and the prig in me were very strong, but I found at last a companion who was minded to follow the same course and he took me to various haunts of his. 'These girls,' he said, ' are not prostitutes or anything like it; they are women who have missed sexual experiences during their earth life and need to work out this lack before they can progress, just as we do. So we are all in the same boat and start equal. You will find some lovely people here.'

Much of my reluctance had left me when Mitchell explained the differences between sexual relationships here and those known on earth. To understand them it is necessary to remember that there has been a total change in the body substance and that the basis of all relationships here is purely emotional. One does not think how handsome, nor how plain another person is but judges them entirely on the quality of their auras or emanations. Where an attraction between the sexes is felt, it is a pure emotion of love and the urge is to draw near and share the warmth and beauty one desires. Lust as such is hardly possible in this plane. If union takes place it is an interfusion of the two bodies and an ecstatic and satisfying experience far more lovely than anything one could experience in an earthly body. There is no question of the procreation of children so that all the more sordid side of the sexual relation is unnecessary.

'You know,' said my friend, 'You are wrong to try and minimise the importance of sexual life. It is one of the problems most men have to solve when they come here. We have to come to terms with a body compacted of emotion and far more highly charged than before. There are other regions where things are done just as on earth although no children are produced. I have known men who have been with us for a time but have been so obsessed with this business that they have elected to go back there because they hankered after the old ways. They will probably find them unsatisfying after a while and will come back to us again, but they have to work it out for themselves.'

We entered a large and friendly gathering of young people and were made welcome. Groups formed and dispersed and there was an air of expectation and excitement about which had its effect on us all. I found a girl who pleased me and who was gracious enough to approve of my company and we were both glad to improve our knowledge of each other. She was small and slight, radiant yet veiled in her own tentativeness. We wandered away together absorbed in comparing our earth experiences and soon we became friendly and comfortable together. I was charmed by the ease of this feminine comradeship: we were both curious and expectant; we both admitted freely our lack of ex-

perience and our need to remedy it, yet we shared a
great diffidence and a sensitive approach.


I did not return to the home for a long while. We two
have wandered happily in an enchanted land exploring the delights of an intimate companionship crowned
by the magic of union. She is very lovely; at her heart
is an innocence, joined to a flame-like ardour and between us we create a burning bliss of union. I am in-
toxicated with happiness and for a time have forgotten
all my problems and difficulties. Without sorrow we
both begin to feel the beginning of the inevitable withdrawal and we have discovered that neither of us had
expected a permanent relationship. This has brought
no disappointment but rather gratitude for a perfect
experience shared. Winifred tells me that she is in
search of her own man, one who had been her elder
and had died early in the century. She suspects that he
has gone on and that her only way of finding him will
be to make progress in her own development. So for
her our idyll has been a means to that end and we are
able to part with no regrets or anything but a great
regard and affection for each other. Blessed girl! I
thank my stars that I have met her and I foresee that
the day it not far distant when she will go on her way
to join her own man.

So we have bidden each other farewell. She returns
to her friends and I find myself back again at the only
home I know. Mitchell is delighted with my improvement and we have talked at length about the ways in

which he wants me to work out my own salvation. I have got beyond resenting his intrusion into my private life. Such an attitude is ruled out by the very conditions under which we live and I know and trust the affection and concern which prompt his interest.

'You have broken down one of your worst inhibitions,' he said to me. 'You can feel for yourself how this release of energy has relieved the tension under which you were living. I think you will also find that the anxiety factor which was an indication of your fear of living has been reduced.'

'I won't even pretend that I didn't enjoy it,' I admitted, 'but I still think that it would have been impossible to me under earth conditions.'

'That, I am afraid, is a symptom of another trouble of yours,' he went on. 'We now have to work at a great weight of distrust and resentment of your kind which is making a dark centre in your being. You need to mix more freely with people and to like them more. You will find this easier here than on earth because on this plane you will meet only congenial people. They have all reached a comparable standard of development.'

Here an objection and withdrawal in my mind jumped the gap between us like an electric spark and he smiled at me in understanding.

'Yes,' he said, 'your big difficulty is a scorn of slowness and impatience of mediocrity and, if you will forgive me, a really horrible feeling of superiority to most of the pleasant and ordinary people you are meeting here. They cannot avoid recognising your reaction to them and so they keep away from you. Now how are we to get that right? I think you really feel that you ought to be able to find and meet the great people of the past whom you would perhaps regard as your equals, but my dear fellow, you are not yet fit to come near them. Look at yourself!'

I looked. Either I saw myself through his eyes or in some kind of immaterial mirror, but this is what I saw: shafts of keen blue light struggling to issue from a core of dark and muddied colour – a tumult of angry, murky shadow at the centre and as a response to his merciless criticism angry dartings of red flying off from it. It was not a pretty sight.

'You see,' he said gently, 'we have to clear all that before you are ready to go on.'

The shock broke me down. All my pride and un-confessed arrogance were shattered. I saw myself as less worthy than the least of these to whom I had been condescending and they must have seen it and known it as clearly as I was doing. At this crisis I fought one of my hardest battles. I subdued the angry response and begged Mitchell to go on helping me and to deal mercilessly with the faults he saw in me. A great flood of affection, warm and healing came from him to me as he replied.

'Thank you for taking it like that. I knew you were big enough to stand the treatment.'

For the first time I was beaten, not by any-thing exterior – that can happen to anyone – but by an intimate revelation of what was within. I was reduced to a state of helpless penitence and pride slunk

out of sight. Mitchell was wise and has left me alone
to recover from this collapse. Eventually I have regained some balance but only by climbing down for
good from my false pedestal and painfully accepting
myself as I am; a mess, a travesty of what I might
have been.

The storm has a little subsided and a strange sense
of relief has come out of this abasement. I feel a new
dignity and a truer integrity than I have ever known.
Perhaps I have reached rock bottom now and there is
rest and peace in that thought.


By such means Mitchell is cleansing and clearing the
darkness of my inner self, a darkness of which I had
never been aware on earth and which in its passing
has shaken and shattered the false personality so long
and so painfully built up during my earth life. But
all this is a long and hard process and as I write it is
still far from complete.

The arbitrary solitude I demanded, with its implied
superiority to human companionship has also to go.
At least I see it now for what it is although I am
still impelled to be alone and crave occasional periods
of quietness. I am still a very young and raw recruit
to this kind of living where the being is unshielded
by the inertia of the physical body. All experiences
here are tried out on the quick of the being and in
their keenness and piercing reality are beyond anything it is possible to feel on earth. My emotions still
shake me dangerously and I have to learn also to take

the emotional impact of other beings with equanimity. I have become wary of impatience and anger; their manifestations are too repulsive. The slightest shift in feeling makes a corresponding change in appearance as well as in one's own feeling of well-being. Relations with people, when nothing can be hidden, become a high art requiring control and a larger sympathy than is ever needed on earth where its absence can usually be covered by the conventional word or action. It really amounts to this, that one is not safe in this plane until all the twisted, negative emotions are cleared out of one. Then it will be possible to live fearlessly and freely knowing that one cannot send out any harmful motion. Hence Mitchell's drastic treatment.

I can see that this kind of living, naked to emotional stress, imposing candour and demanding innocence, cannot be successfully carried out without training. During my earth life I had never bothered overmuch to cultivate the art of human relationships so now I have the more to learn. Of course I am not the only one; at the home we are all learning much the same lessons and I find myself often 'bottom of the form'. Mitchell is endlessly patient with us when control slips and impatience or anger fume out of us. He knows how to take the horrid emanations into his own clear being and transform them there. If he returned them in kind the resulting state of all of us would not bear thinking of; it would no doubt approximate to the state of the gloomy town I had cause to remember too well. But in thus accepting and transforming the waves of negative emotion we sometimes send out he shames us into fresh effort. For he suffers. The delicate fabric of his body is harmed and hurt although he tries not to flinch when he is scorched by our beastly reactions. By degrees we are learning our lesson and if control threatens to slip we go away by ourselves so that no one else needs to endure our nastiness. The conviction is brought home to us that unless we can clear ourselves of evil emotions it will not be possible for us to remain among the decent people on this plane. The alternative will be to leave it and find homes in conditions where the astral bodies of the inhabitants are coarsened by habitual indulgence in anger and hatred and where the air they breathe is infected with their hot and murky emanations. I have already had a glimpse of these dark conditions and can imagine the misery of being condemned to stay there for any length of time.

As my own state improves courage and cheerfulness are returning and the spirit of fun sparkles out more often. I begin to experience the kind of happiness possible here; clean, clear sparkling living, a purity and sweetness never to be known by an earth-clogged consciousness. All joys, as indeed all sorrows, are keener; just as joy can irradiate so sorrow can pierce like a sword. It is not easy to keep a balance between these sharply contrasted emotions and there are backslidings when perhaps one of us disappears for a while to find in solitude a solution to some personal problem or to wait for the coming of a better attitude. But in spite of set-backs we improve and each victory earns us richer, fuller happiness. All the time life is opening up into fresh vistas of joyful experience. The exhilaration of the promise it holds bears us up over the rougher parts of the journey.

# Chapter 3

SOWING AND REAPING

A GOOD DEAL of suffering is caused among us by the memories of our past which continually recur to remind us of mistakes or crimes. It seems that an earth-consciousness can tolerate the thought of wrong-doing and find excuses for it which ease the mind; one can learn to live with one's mistakes and can be satisfied to cover up one's crimes. Here we have to know and feel more keenly the things we have done; we can no longer ignore the point of view of the man we have injured and we have actually to experience what he felt in the matter as though we had ourselves been the sufferer. On earth, most of us lack the imagination to do this or we might be held back from many of the blindly ruthless actions we do. Imagination now takes a more poignant form; we have intimately to experience the other's suffering.

So one of our hardest tasks is to come to terms with our own past misdeeds. Mitchell tells me that had we stayed on a lower plane where the make-up of our bodies would have remained coarser and less sensitive many of these old errors would not have caused us any distress. We should have tolerated the memories of them almost as easily as we seem to have done on earth. But in this plane our more sensitive bodies which are so easily shaken by emotion cannot easily sustain the guilt and suffering left behind by such experiences.

This is the longest and most painful part of our progress. How to think rightly of what in our ignorance and hardness of heart we have done amiss; how to reconcile ourselves to the wounds we have dealt others and now have to feel in our own being? This is the new aspect of wrongdoing which we have to face, for inasmuch as I have injured another I now have to suffer his pain. It is really an illustration of the solidarity of mankind and proof that every deed affects the whole as well as the part.

I myself am tormented particularly by an incident of my war years. It caused me infinite distress at the time, but now the agony of realisation I am enduring is in proportion to my keener powers of feeling. During guerilla warfare in the desert I had thought it my duty to condemn a man for conduct likely to imperil the campaign. Justice demanded, I thought, that if I passed sentence I must carry it out myself. So, under the pretext of military necessity, I murdered that man. Moreover, I bungled the job and so protracted his suffering. Although at the time I could see no other course, I know now that my poverty of imagination and resource drove me to this. Now I have to endure all that I did to him; not only the physical suffering – the smallest part of it – but I have to know his despair and remorse and the awful blow to pride and affection inflicted by my condemnation.

My first overpowering impulse was to go in search of him and make what reparation I could but Mitchell has checked me and shown me that there is no solution that way.

'Even if you could find him and could ease your own present hurt you would still fail to undo the past,' he said. I groaned and admitted that he was right. After a silence, Mitchell continued: 'You caused the suffering the extent of which you now know for the first time. This is your share of that suffering. Because you are capable of keen feeling your share may well be the greater. Can you accept this as the consequence of a wrong train of events set going at a moment of your earthly life by this man and carried on to a wrong conclusion by you? Pick up this cross, this consequence, and carry it willingly. It is yours; you made it.'

It seemed to me at that moment that I could not bear it, but I approved Mitchell's dealings with me. He admitted no excuse and suggested no palliative. He made me take the full weight of it and at the same time gave me confidence in my power to carry it.

There was virtue in that. Not all at once but little by little I find my pain is decreasing. Mitchell said to me: 'Thank God you have no worse crimes to cope with. Will you think with compassion of what is in store for major wrong-doers? Even if at first they are so hardened by crime that they can bear to stay in places where, because of the kind of company they keep they can bear to live with themselves, yet sooner or later the process of purification will begin and they will have to come here. Then their future progress will inevitably bring them face to face with their crimes in this painful and inescapable form. What about the justice of God now?'

Submission to this justice has brought to me a special peace and stability. I know that a dark place in my being has been cleansed and the remorse lurking there has been purged away. I realise with reflected agony what I did, I see myself as the criminal idiot who could do a thing like that and through this abasement I have gained a truer knowledge of myself. I do not know how to describe adequately the relief, the lucidity the new vigour that has succeeded this purgation. I am finding out what it is to rest on a basis of humility with all pretensions to superiority, cleverness and wisdom burnt out of me.

Of course there are many other unhappy things in my past that I shall have to know, suffer and accept in the same way. Each will bring its own meed of retributive suffering, each will teach me the measure of my real stature and bring me nearer to humility and peace. As Mitchell remarks, this process of purgation

is the justification of the Catholic doctrine of purga-
tory, although its discipline is mental and emotional
instead of physical. Yet emotion for us is really physical, so perhaps red-hot pincers and so on are not so in-
appropriate as symbols.

All this process is going on in the context of everyday living. We are not always sorrowing for our sins,
yet the memories of our past recur in consciousness
and we cannot escape from them for long. We have to
get them into proper relation with our estimate of ourselves, to expiate wrong-doing by our own pain, and to
integrate the whole experience into the new self we are
building up. This for me means the destruction of the
false self and the facing and acceptance of the real.
When all scores are cleared we shall be free to go on.

Time is passing over and it is already some years
in earth reckoning since I came here. The unrestricted
flow of our time, freed from the exterior standards of
day and night, winter and summer, is difficult to
measure, but I know that the process of purification is
a lengthy one. It cannot be hurried or carried out to
any schedule because the material from the past comes
to the surface of consciousness in its own time and
cannot be dealt with until this happens. I shall stay
here with Mitchell as long as he advises it and indeed
I am not anxious to go on until I have gained more
control and confidence. Joys and sorrows are balanced
here. It is sometimes a giddy exchange since both have
a poignancy which I cannot hope to describe and the
drop from the heights to the depths rocks the mind to
its foundations. But Mitchell assures us that the storms

will pass and that we shall attain equilibrium in a deeper and more permanent happiness than we can as yet imagine. Looking at him, we know that this must be true.

# Chapter 4

EXPLORING

OUR LIFE HERE is many-sided and in spite of its new
and absorbing interests most of us retain a lively concern with earthlife. There are backward glances and in
some quarters a great interest in those not always reliable sources of information provided by what are
called 'mediums'. A peculiar and eventually valuable
experience of this sort came my way some time ago. I
knew that some of my friends had means of making
contact with earth and out of curiosity I went one day
with several others to a place where they thought they
could get in touch with a medium. This was not one
of the usual arrangements where a person on this plane
who had perfected communication with a medium
could control her physical organism and pass messages

through her to and from earth. Such arrangements are usually well organised on this side and some degree of accuracy may be hoped for. In this unusual case a spirit in the throes of a cataclysm of emotion had somehow broken through into communication with this sphere and the phenomenon had aroused some curiosity. I went to see for myself.

I realised that this poor soul was suffering great mental distress because of her ignorance of our conditions and her inability to trust the sporadic fragments which were reaching her. We did not know how much of our words and thoughts she was picking up and she had no guarantee that her attempts to reach us were succeeding. I was moved to help and persuaded the others to leave the job to me for the time being. After a great many patient efforts I succeeded in getting a clear message to her for the first time and she was at last convinced that she was in touch with a real person. I shared in her joy and relief. Unsafeguarded, she had made a perilous venture and in its earlier stages had unfortunately made dangerous contacts with those on a lower plane. Interference from them often confused our earlier attempts, since the medium herself had no means of knowing with whom she was in touch, but by degrees we 'cleared the line'.

We found more reliable ways of communicating; almost by accident we hit on the method of automatic writing. She sat one day with her pen in her hand. I sent an urgent thought which surprisingly her pen transcribed. She told me she had been trying to get automatic writing for years but without success, but

to me it was a novel experience to find that when I
wrote down an idea she reproduced it faithfully on
her paper, and not only that, but the writing was a
facsimile of my own. On occasions she also picked up
my words as I spoke them, but we both trusted the
method of writing and usually fell back on it. I got
glimpses of her and soon found out as much about her
life and interests as she did about mine. I made use of
her too, for it happened from time to time that public
reference would be made to my name or deeds and I
could follow through her the strange developments of
my earthly fame. She even read to me books written
by my friends and I saw afresh through her eyes the
records of campaigns I had myself written.

In my struggles with my past all this had its place
and was of immense value to me. Our friendship continued, but my medium friend soon after was able to
get in touch with her husband whom she had really
been seeking when I first found her. He and I later on
collaborated with her and formed a little group to
speak and write together. She was full of questioning
not only about our actual life here but about a wider
system of ideas which might relate what we told her
of it to what she could contribute about earth life.
Naturally we started some insoluble problems but we
got very intrigued with the system of ideas which was
building up and felt we were making some contribu-
tion to a better understanding of our mutual problems.
We were often at a loss, however, and as though in
answer to our perplexities there was eventually an interposition from a higher sphere by an intelligence we

all learned to love and trust and soon there were three of us working with her and helping to fit together the knowledge of earth and of the spheres. I found this absorbing and while I added my quota of knowledge and experience I was finding connections and understanding which helped me to adjust to my own fate.

In addition to this continuing interest, other activities now claim some of my time. I have succeeded in finding a few of my old friends. As Mitchell helped me, so I am able in my turn to help them to adjust to this new world. There are sorrowful occasions when I have to admit that my help is for the time being useless and that they must be left to work their way upward in their own time. I have found out how to get back to the dreary regions where once I was lost and now and again I am able to guide a wanderer to a better place. Not that all souls have to pass through this Hades as I did; many are better prepared and come straight through to the light.

Toleration of these lower conditions is hard for me, however, and my endurance of them is short-lived. Living in the pure air and brightness of this sphere it is harder than ever to endure the murk and gloom. I have made a few returns and effected a few rescues, but now I have left this work to those who are more practised in it and am following my real interest, a continuation of my life-long concern with the Arabs and their life.

In this plane are to be found replicas of earth with all its races and countries and by exercising the wonderful power of desire one can travel and explore at will. I want to find again some of those who fought with me and suffered and endured in those desert campaigns. I cannot know how many of my old comrades will be found on these planes and this has to wait until I can explore the terrain. One after another they come back into my mind and I long to see them and to know that all is well with them. So I shall set out.

I went to the coast, a coast corresponding in its features to the rugged cliffs of England and there I took ship. Yes, there are ships here just as there are houses and towns. Voyages are easier; no mischance can occur and the direction is assured by the purpose and desire of the voyagers. Our journey has not been a lengthy business of calling at port after port so we have soon reached our destination and I find myself again in a country which is the counterpart of Egypt. There are significant differences. Instead of the loafers and beggars and the dirt and smells of the East as I remember it here is a clean and smiling land but one which appears to have a very small population. I have seen no familiar face but all those I meet are friendly and happy souls. The slums and filth of the old towns have gone but so have most of the people. This is a dream city and I have left it and am out in the clear air of the desert again. Travelling on foot is no hardship; fatigue is never felt and desire impels one swiftly and surely onward.

The desert has all and more than its remembered beauty but none of its terrors. It is not possible to get lost and hunger and thirst can no longer prove one's undoing since one can go on indefinitely without food or drink. I am revelling in the clean, bare land and savouring again the desert air with its piercing purity. Lovely to be free also from dependence upon a surly camel, a train of followers and all the tiresome paraphernalia necessary in the old days to keep one alive.

I have recalled many of the strange and romantic places I once knew and have found their counterparts here. They are for the most part lonely and deserted. The clean emptiness and peace of the desert seem to have flowed in over all traces of man's occupation and to have obliterated his soiling mark. The silence, the solitude, judge me and I know myself to be unworthy. I can recall only one soul who might be attuned to these awful simplicities, a wandering, ragged holy man whom I once met in some such conditions on earth. He had the soul of a child, of a fanatic; he was mad, or else so sane as to shame others into calling him mad. He, I thought, may well be at home here where he will find an easier approach to the vision of the infinite which possessed him.

So thinking, I had climbed a rocky eminence when I came upon him. This should not have surprised me, since my thought had led me to him. His radiance warmed, pierced and enlightened me so that I could not approach him closely. We did not speak; words would have been an impertinence in that place; but a light of love and understanding flashed between us and I too entered into that holy of holies where he communed with God. Too pure and rarified the air on this mountain top for me to bear for long. Soon I left him, still transfixed in worship, and went on my way.

Many places I have visited, some few of my companions I have found and spoken with. Now that I have partly destroyed the barriers which always used to defend my miserable citadel of self, intercourse with my friends is becoming an easy joy, an unfolding and sharing which enriches and satisfies. There is little need of words; a kind of communion of thought and feeling takes their place and the lovely tides of human trust and affection flow freely between us who had always felt the ties of brotherhood.

These are the few. There are many whom I cannot trace. They must be making their way onwards by their own paths. I know enough now of the majestic order and progress by which human life ascends to be content to leave these men in the hands of their own fate. It will infallibly bring them in time to whatever sphere represents the limit of their possible striving.

The East holds me in as strong a web of attraction as ever and I have wandered here for long; years, perhaps, because time, like space takes on a different quality here. All arbitrary and exterior standards are gone and time and space are felt in direct relationship to one's present experience. There are no words to tell what this has meant to me in enlargement and purification. I begin to know beyond all telling what is meant by fulness of life, life of a vital quality which expands to take in the whole of creation and finds it good.

At last I have returned to my own place. During my long absence there have been changes and I find my world altered in many ways. The men in the home are different and having greeted Mitchell and talked with him I have gone off to my own cottage and have settled down to do some thinking. I begin to feel it necessary to make a more intensive study of the conditions of life here. Up to the present I have gone hither and thither blundering into new circumstances and doing the best I could with them, learning from experience something of the make and powers of the human psyche and realising new aspects of experience. Now I feel the necessity to fit all these odd adventures into novelty together and to attempt to make a whole of them. My earth life already feels more than a lifetime away; remote and unreal and its cramping frustrating necessities just a bad dream. Day and night, cold and heat, inescapable hunger and thirst – all these have vanished out of existence. Here we still have a material aspect of life but it wears an easier air; hard necessities of an exterior kind are relaxed or non-existent.

But with this change another set of inexorables has come into view. The world which has now to be conquered is the interior world of the emotions and the spirit. Before, one avoided physical suffering if possible and endured it with what courage one might if it was inevitable. Now, suffering is of the soul and the spirit and cannot be avoided if it has been incurred. It too has to be borne with fortitude and in time and with help cured. Just as on earth one speedily learned that fire burned, hard things hurt and sharp things cut and there were limits to human strength and prowess, so here a whole new set of rules of conduct has to be mastered. There is, in fact, a framework of moral law as rigid as the framework of physical law for earth. On earth I think it is beginning to be suspected that the rule of law goes beyond the physical but there is no peradventure about it for us; it has become a matter of daily experience. One had better know and observe the rules so as not to get hurt. Although law is thus transposed from a physical basis to a moral one, it still operates in physical ways. Emotions are a visible and tangible reality forming a good or bad body, healthy or diseased according to one's state. If one is diseased and repulsive one cannot hide the fact but must submit to treatment.

Emotions, as well as forming the stuff of our bodies, can be used as a very real force. They can be sent out from the body with almost lethal effect and the discharge of hatred, anger or cruelty can cause grievous injury to the one against whom it is directed. In fact, there is no longer any need to moralise about such things; they are no longer in the realm of the abstract, but are open and palpable offences for which a penalty must be paid. Society is organised on a basis of emotional health; the angry, the sadistic, the brutal and the jealous have of necessity to foregather in their own place, because the atmosphere they engender cannot be borne by others, nor can they themselves bear the more rarified conditions of the higher spheres. Cure of these disorders comes gradually and as they are cured

men are able to graduate into better conditions and
are admitted to higher planes of being. It is a caste
system if you like, but one based on fundamental
affinities and never a cast-iron system from which there
is no escape. The path upward is always open and
there are willing hands to help and encourage any
man who aspires to tread it.

But just as on earth the soul begins to grow and fills
the being with strange and unwonted desires, so now
the developing spirit forming within this body of
desire, creates an unrest and a longing for a yet higher
mode of being. The shackles of time are removed it is
true, so that the period we need for growth can be
long or short. This phase of living is not bounded by
any 'three score years and ten', nor does a decaying
physique put a period to development as so often it
does on earth. My time is my own and I can have as
much of it as I need; another example of the relaxa-
tion of tension and the easing of conditions.

I have hinted on several occasions that the mode of
communication here is not confined to the utterance of
words. One never needs to express in words one's feeling for another. It is always apparent in the immediate reaction of one's body and cannot fail to be
read correctly. Where there is affection and trust there
will be an outflowing of warmth and light; where there
is polite indifference as when one meets a stranger the
auric colour will continue steady and unaffected by the
encounter; dislike or contempt cannot be hidden; they
will flow out in waves of confused and muddy colour
pleasant neither to see nor to feel upon one's sensitive

body. So the immediate feeling will always be fully apparent and will need no words.

The transmission of meaning involves not the emotional body alone but the as-yet imperfectly formed spiritual body. Where there is affinity of spirit and closeness of emotional regard meaning is often carried between friends without the clumsy intervention of words. It 'jumps the gap' and is immediately and fully apprehended as it could never be if it had to be trimmed to fit a pattern of words.

Words are most useful in everyday and trivial matters and they continue to be used whenever necessary. Our independence of language is only partial but it is enough to make us realise the artificiality of language barriers. When you can *see* the feelings of a man of different race far more clearly than you can see his 'colour' and you know from this that he is friendly and interested; when you can also exchange enough meaning to prove the kinship of your minds then the obstacle of language is defeated and the fatal misunderstandings due to ineffectual exchanges in words are avoided.

I am ashamed now to remember that on earth I had great difficulty in my relationships with men whom I then regarded as inferior. I cultivated an attitude of fastidiousness which allowed me to regard them as less than human. One of my problems here has been to correct this attitude. My earlier experiences in the city of gloom brought me into touch with such men and women and I had shrunk in horror from any contact with them. Now I am learning that all of these

are on their way upwards and will in time stand where
I stand now and that their faults and failings will exact
from them, alas, the just measure of suffering. Moreover, the adjustment of my own place in the scale of
things has given me a different standard. I see now
that I was like Shakespeare's dreamer 'a king of infinite space' but 'Waking, no such thing'. With every
advantage of education and upbringing I brought with
me so much evil, weakness and wrong thinking and
have had to be cured of it through so much pain and
shame that I can have nothing but compassion and
respect in my heart now for these others. My hiararchy
of human values has had to be altered: instead of the
imperfect judgements of earth where an adding up of
this and that gives only an arbitrary and superficial
result, here one sees a man clearly and as a whole. My
friend Mitchell is one of the finest men I know here.
He is clean, clear, controlled and beautiful. Yet one
day he showed me a man who will be his superior. He
took me to a gloomy region where he needed my help.
There we found a man, lost as I once had been. His
being glowed with power and darted out brilliant rays
of blue and purple, the colours of a high spiritual development, but he was enveloped in a cloud of anger
and despair and at the heart of him was a black and
composite nucleus of evil. We found him difficult to
approach; twice we were driven back choking with his
emanations and at first he spurned our help. Mitchell
told me afterwards that this was a great if erring soul
beside whom any of us would be small and feeble once
he was cured of his infirmities. I am intensely in-

terested and shall follow his course. He has had no
fame or fortune on earth; he might well have been one
of those whom I should have despised; yet potentially
he is one of the great ones.

One's scale of values has to be graded not upon
present conditions but upon potential being; not what
one is, but what one is capable of becoming is the
criterion now. Greatness may therefore be found in the
most unhappy and evil-ridden of men. I have also to
revise my attitude to women for now I have to see
the wonderful qualities of love and sympathy they
often possess. Their quiet strength and power of endurance is also a revelation to me. I suppose I had
always refused to see this on earth, preferring to stress
their vanity and futility. But these are small failings
here; they scarcely dim the radiance of love which
shines from many a humble woman soul. Indeed, the
great lady is often de-graded in favour of her poorer
sister, for real value is a great leveller. All the nonsense of social standards is lost sight of here because
we have to see the true nature of each one and to
recognise that social grade has very little to do with it.
In fact, the queen and the peasant sometimes, though
not always, have to change places. How cleverly good
looks and social standing often mask a poverty-
stricken and desiccated soul on earth! One certainty
gets a great many surprises as well as gives them, no
doubt.

The levelling tendencies operating increasingly in
human society on earth look at first like a reflection
of this process, but what goes wrong on earth is that

the classes are reversed so that one or the other level claims a monopoly of all the virtues. Here, we find that the stratification of society runs vertically through the usual orders and so our 'noblemen' may come with equal likelihood from any social level.

The real 'classes' into which we are separated are divided in space because they have to obey the primal law of affinity. Near and far mean likeness or difference in development and there is a compulsion in the association of groups of similar levels. Each group makes its own conditions and these are for the time being the only conditions in which its members can exist in comfort. Whatever our natural plane may be, to go down from it causes acute discomfort and even suffering; to go up before one is ready means an air too rarefied and light too intense to be borne. So each must go to his own place and stay there until development draws him up into a higher sphere.

# Chapter 5

ADVENTURES IN THE WORLD OF
THOUGHT

I BEGIN NOW to get a wider notion of the whole process
of development by which men move towards their own
fulfilment. It is a vast and slow-moving progress and
for a long while I could see only a small part of it.
The expansion of outlook as the actual 'scheme of
salvation' unfolds itself is gradual and inevitable. First
comes the knowledge that life is indeed indestructible,
then the stern experience that each soul goes inevitably to its own place, and, lastly, the realisation that
no man is damned however he may be warped by evil
but that by effort and suffering he can free himself
from it and develop to the highest level of which he is
capable.

Meanwhile, sitting in my cottage thinking and writing, I began to get intimations that I was not thinking alone. In the pauses of my own thinking an opening of clarity and illumination seemed to be made in my mind to admit a flow of larger ideas. This was a lovely experience and I gave myself up to it. I got a clear impression of a kind of conference in which several people were exchanging ideas and developing them in ways that interested me. Almost involuntarily, I found myself asking questions which were considered and answered and then it dawned on me that one of the participants was my medium friend and that I was in touch with the group I have mentioned before. Again the principle of affinity leads to unexpected encounters and bears no relation to physical distance. In this group there was one earth-dweller, two of us on this plane and one on a higher plane and although none was in the bodily presence of another a satisfactory way of communicating had been evolved, simply on the basis of affinity. After joining in in this disembodied way once or twice, I have sought out the medium's husband, Andrew, who is on this plane and therefore accessible to me and he has encouraged me to go on co-operating with them. I explained to him how I had 'overheard' their conversation and he has told me more about this higher intelligence which has been contacted. Each gets into communication with the medium independently whichever plane they work from. So I have joined their group and am working with them either by finding their thought while sitting quietly in my cottage or sometimes by finding Andrew and sharing the experience with him. The four of us have been working out a theory which covers the facts as we know them, both here and on earth.

The experience of sharing the thought of others who are not present with me opens up a whole vista of new possibilities. Think of it! One is part of a great universe of thought which can be tapped without the mechanical interchange of words, either heard or read. It fascinates me more than any of the new powers of this wonderful life. I have been deliberately experimenting and trying to reach the thoughts of other minds, especially those who most inspired me on earth. Sometimes I succeed, sometimes I fail. I am, of course, finding out that there is nothing haphazard about this process but that it follows strict rules. As one might expect, the basic law is affinity. One can only hope to contact minds with which one has or could have had affinity, a relationship of kind with kind, however different in development. Appreciation of a poet or writer may argue a certain degree of affinity but that particular soul may have progressed beyond one's reach and so one draws a blank. On the contrary, in rare cases he may have retrogressed. Then there are other conditions that must be satisfied. There has to be a congruence of thought at the same time. If, for instance, I try to find a mind which I associate with a certain type of thought and at that particular time that mind is occupied with matters of a different nature then no contact is likely to be made. Barriers can deliberately be created when one is set against communication and then a kind of darkness intervenes to cut off any transmission. But this free and roving adventure of the mind at large in the world of thought has come to mean a great deal to me and serves as a re-education in the new values I have to learn. Not only this, but it gives me also a pure and endless source of joy because at rare intervals my world opens into vistas of a larger, freer life and experience – a wonder of light and joy beyond telling.

Pursuing these new avenues of experience I have hugged my solitude and almost resent the coming of a chance guest. But Mitchell, who never forgets me for long has come in search of me and to him I have opened all this. We have had a long talk and he has, I am sure, counselled me wisely although I am reluctant to take his advice. He warns me that if I continue to follow this solitary way of living and to use my time trying to share the experiences of my betters I shall make no progress and may even regress so that higher experiences will become closed to me. I am afraid that he is right and that I must get out and mingle more with my fellows. Interludes of mental adventure are permissible so long as they are balanced by activity.

This brings me up against a problem which has been at the root of the restlessness and failure of my earth life. I understand only too well the joys of solitude and savour them here, as there. I have always known too, the joy of activity and supremely so in my early days of active campaigning. Then I had the power to plan and initiate action and a delight in my influence over men and events. The two sides of my nature were always at war, however, and life never gave me the opportunity to resolve the conflict, or perhaps I myself was too blind and weak to see it in proper perspective then. Doubts, disappointments and failures sapped belief in my power to act effectively, and in the end I gave up the struggle and abdicated, giving over the ordering of my active life to others and reserving only my private life as the sphere of self-government. In this capitulation I found peace of a kind but it perpetuated the division in my being and was no real solution.

So I have brought the problem here and as I come to terms with the more obvious aspects of life here so sooner or later this problem is bound to come uppermost. For a while I have been able to skulk in my cottage and avoid the issue but after my conversation with Mitchell I know that I must face the dilemma. Part of my being thirsts for action, responsible action; part craves the irresponsible bliss of mental freedom only to be achieved in solitude.

Mitchell has made me see that I have to find a way of life that will fulfil both parts of my nature and the despairing thing is that I seem to have lost the desire and the power to initiate action. The wish to do so is numb and paralysed yet a fever of impatience with the not-doing makes a chaos in my being. I look around on this ordered, happy world and can find nowhere any stimulus to action. True, there is work to be done but except I place myself under orders and go about it as a will-less instrument it will not be done by me.

Mitchell sets his face against any such compromise.

He says that only by finding a task which seems peculiarly my own can I work out my salvation at this difficult stage. He counsels patience and a quiet persistence in meeting and co-operating with others until I find my own path. Meanwhile, and in the intervals of following his advice I shall continue to interest myself in the work going on with the group and the medium I mentioned before since this is at least a profitable use for my time.

The battle is raging within me, nevertheless, and I have bouts of despair when it seems that the warring elements will again produce a deadlock as they did on earth. The stale distaste for any course of action I seem able to envisage returns upon me whenever I am goaded by impatience with my inactivity. My suffering is real enough and there is a great temptation to give up the battle and sink into the defeated life of the solitary. If I do this I can be happy after a fashion, as I well know, but it will mean a permanent self-stultification. More, I shall have intensified the pattern of conflict ending in the defeat of my active self and again I know too well the despair and suicide of hope this brings with it. I begin to understand how vital this crisis of decision is. On earth I once faced the same crisis only then in bewilderment and futility; now it comes back upon me, as all such unresolved conflicts must, but now I can see it set out clear and stark. I am compounded of two elements, each strongly charged and hard to control; they tear me between them unless I bludgeon one or the other into submission. This is no solution and I know it. At least I can now see the dilemma truly and I know what I have to do: I have to find in myself the urge to live in a way which will satisfy both.

Turning idly over my earth memories, my mind has lit up a particular series. In the intervals of active service and among other ways of filling the waste of life since those days I had always a great interest in the actual making of books, in their printing and format. This has come to me as an inspiration and perhaps will provide me with the opening into activity for which I am searching. I do not know anyone here who can put me in the way of such work, but sitting in my cottage trying to sort out this problem of work I feel strongly that here may be a solution. The art of making books is as much needed here as on earth and my imagination takes fire at the opening of far richer possibilities than I could have found on earth. Think of the books I could make here! Clean, clear, lovely print, paper worthy of it and bindings of a rich splendour seemly to the substance of the book. Thus dreaming, I have left the cottage and gone abroad trusting to be led to the places where such crafts are followed.


I have wandered far from my own countryside and have found an ancient city where are seats of learning; not an exact replica of my own Oxford but a university town of widely-spaced buildings of noble aspect. At a distance across meadows there arose a grey tower of many storeys and towards this I went. At its base I came upon a man I had once known slightly, to our mutual pleasure, and after a kind greeting he has taken me to his rooms. All this is like, but yet unlike, the university life I used to know and I find myself among very choice spirits who have made me welcome and are urging me to stay among them. But I am still fired by my purpose and shall not rest until I have found a fellow enthusiast.

I have found my man. Thomas is a quiet, studious soul but at the mention of book-making he was transformed. He led me away to his workshop and press and here are all the familiar tools of his art only of better make and adapted to finer ends than any I have had the joy of handling before. We soon were deep in the technicalities of his craft and I have been welcomed as a learner and helper. Books are still needed, books are still being written and read and studied but they are not being turned out in the senseless and shoddy profusion of earth. Such books as are being produced, fruits of wit, wisdom and love of beauty are being handled with a care and skill of craftsmanship which delight me.

My cottage is forgotten and I have thrown myself whole-heartedly into the work. We labour for the joy of it and for as long or short a time as the joy lasts. We keep no journeyman hours here and the lack of the regular punctuation of time into day and night is a great freedom to us. In this cool, green-shaded workroom I am learning many new arts of engraving, printing and tooling and in the pleasure of the hand and the exultation of seeing that the work is good I am finding full satisfaction. My mind keeps pace with my hands in profitable thinking and I seem at last to have found a recipe for peace.

I am also finding the fulfilment of worthy companionship. These men and women at the university are sometimes my peers but more often my superiors and among us the pure springs of happy activity overflow in fun and sparkling humour. I begin to savour a fulness of life I have never attained before.

An amusing circumstance and one that is giving me much secret satisfaction is that I appear to be approaching my 'proper' age. This is a phenomenon of which Mitchell warned me. It seems that every human being has a true meridian of age at which his being is unfolded at its peak of achievement. For some, it is youth; for some, a riper middle age; for others, even an advanced age. Whichever manifestation of the being was most full and characteristic, at this age the man or woman rests. So it matters not at what age in earthly reckoning a man dies, he reverts by degrees to his ideal age when he comes here. Most of the persons I meet seem to be young but there is an admixture of the mature and elderly. My own experiences have been stormy and troubled but now that I am finding peace and fulfilment I am intrigued to see that I am definitely becoming younger, not only in appearance but in feeling and in my way of relating myself to others. Thomas teases me with the prospect of going right back to childhood and even suggests that the process may not stop there; actually I have achieved equilibrium at about twenty-eight and shall stay there very thankfully. I am young and have the vigour and enthusiasm proper to what is obviously my real age and now can hardly envisage being any older.

Another astonishing change has reconciled me to any loss of the prestige of a riper age. A small man suffers from his lack of inches and is influenced by it in many undesirable ways. He is impelled to try and compensate for it and often does so ruthlessly, to his own and other people's hurt. However great in spirit, he will hardly ever feel safe enough to forgo the defences he builds around his puniness. In my own case, my proper growth was stunted by an accident in youth and so my small stature was only incidental to my form. To my great joy this disability is removed and I have now attained a normal height. Only one who has endured this handicap will realise what a deep satisfaction this is to my vanity. So here I am, young, tall and much more free from the corroding emanations which used to hamper me. I am happily occupied and engaged with congenial companions in a satisfying and useful life. But that I know that I still have far to go I should be full of complacency. This freedom, this satisfaction, this sheer joy of living fill me to the brim with a surging energy of being I could never know before.

# Chapter 6

## THE UNIVERSITY: A TRANSITION

AMONG THE STUDENTS in this university is a young man to whom I am strongly attracted. He is reading the higher philosophy which here takes the place of that studied on earth, for naturally the possession of added knowledge makes radical changes in the premises upon which knowledge is built. The mere fact of survival establishes a new basis of fact and negatives all the materialistic hypotheses about which there is such endless and futile argument on earth. So a whole new edifice of knowledge has to be built not only in philosophy but also in science. We have a new range of 'physical' substances to study which include many that are denied a concrete existence at all on earth. The novel range of their

70

relationships gives rise also to a new mathematics.

So a lifetime of adventure of the mind is opened up for us with new horizons and inexhaustible possibilities. My new friend is absorbed in studies which include much that would be scorned as moonshine and metaphysics on earth but which to us with our new terms of reference is inescapable reality. I am ruefully amused at the inhibitions of thought and imagination I brought with me from earth. Most of these I have had to shed. Having overpassed these limits I am no longer ready with scorn for speculative thought. Ingram's researches, therefore, fascinate me and I am beginning to share his interests.

We talk endlessly and our arguments cover a whole universe of discourse. I look back on my chequered life on earth, so curiously woven of aspirations, achievements, failures and despairs. I link it with the story as it has continued here through diverse episodes of self-realisation and of reborn hope and courage. I can begin to see the two parts of my life as one whole having a recognisable pattern running through them. Having to accept the fact that life is indestructible I am driven to admit that I cannot postulate a beginning if I cannot assert an end. We know that life, whatever in essence it may prove to be, has no end in time; it seems unlikely then, to have had a beginning in time. Like energy, life seems able to take many forms, but its sum remains a constant. If the soul and spirit of a man continue after they emerge from interaction with matter, as is not in question for us, then they almost certainly existed before this interaction with matter.

As to the argument that is so often advanced on earth that soul and spirit are just a by-product of chemical processes in matter, the mere fact of our existence makes nonsense of such a claim. The real puzzle is that soul and spirit, existing upon a higher plane than matter, can and do interact with matter during our earth life. This is the thing *we* feel inclined to be sceptical about!

We have gone on from these thoughts to considering the tenets of re-incarnation as they are taught by a considerable body of the faculty in the university. There is a divided body of opinion on this, one of the most controversial subjects, and many variants of the theory of rebirth are expounded and argued among us. We have to take yet another fact into account; we know that changes will take place in these our new bodies to fit us for life in higher spheres and we realise that the same process must be repeated as one goes higher. Where does it end? Do all those who leave this sphere go higher? Do they continue the upward journey or is there a limit to growth and what sets this limit? These are some of the questions which bring us up against the limitations of our knowledge and may have to wait for further experience before they find answers.

I have had recourse to my old habit of contacting minds on other planes and getting from them evidence for the process I suspect runs through it all. It is clear to me that understanding of these mysteries is dependent upon the state of one's being and that in each successive sphere a wider understanding will dawn, but the insatiable craving for knowledge is not to be fobbed off by such considerations, and even at my lowly stage I am resolved to master as much as I can.

Ingram has not yet developed the power to find and speak with entities not of his own sphere and he was at first sceptical, but I have induced him to sit with me and he puts his own questions to the intelligences we contact. Their replies have convinced him of their possession of knowledge and wisdom beyond our capacity.

In one of these spells of work we got in touch with the group working with the medium I mentioned before and as they were also discussing the subject uppermost in our thought at the moment we sat in and profited by their work. This was not a coincidence, of course; the same subject held our thought and so drew us towards any centre where it was strongly represented. In fact, there is nothing fortuitous about the exchange of thought; just as our bodies are drawn in the direction of our desire, so our minds range the world of thought and centre down wherever they find affinity. This is a fluid state of being very difficult to explain until one has experienced it but it means freedom, richness of experience and the stimulus of constant interchange of ideas. That is in parenthesis; on this first occasion of our encountering the thought of the group Ingram suddenly arrested my hand as I was taking down a reply from the person who is known as 'E.K.'

'I know that man,' he said. 'He is sometimes at the

university giving lectures. I should regard any of his conclusions with great respect.'

'Is there any chance of meeting him?' I asked Ingram.

'It may not be easy,' he said. 'He is not one of the faculty but comes from a higher seat of learning.'

For the moment I have put by the hope of meeting E.K. in the flesh but am the more resolved to follow as closely as I can the work on reincarnation he is doing with our medium. Since this work is intended for earth-dwellers it has a slant which for us is unnecessary. All the arguments for survival itself which may be important to those on earth are redundant as far as we are concerned, but E.K. is nothing if not thorough and the theory of rebirth in his hands is being followed into all its implications in a far-reaching way which delights me. Some of our questions on aspects of the subject which we cannot as yet prove from observation in this sphere are being answered and in such a way that the follow-through of the process from sphere to sphere is a convincingly logical process.

I do not think I have ever been remarkably credulous, either during earth life, or here; in fact, I have probably erred in the other direction. The shock of finding that I had survived what I had believed to be the final extinction of being had certainly shaken me and awakened my mind to many possibilities I should previously have scouted. But something must also be allowed for the different quality of our minds; our intelligence is more lighted, open as never before to new impressions. Minds have a clarity, a fluent activity which like our light and facile bodies is in itself a source of delight. The numbing weight of matter being removed we are free to travel mentally into more adventurous paths of speculation which before we might have scorned. Freedom, illumination, a more flexible mental equipment – all help us to go out fearlessly for all knowledge within our scope. It is a magical world of singing vitality and freedom.

I am now embarked on a full and busy life in which I print, bind and tool handsome books in Thomas' peaceful company, and spend much time in happy companionship and fruitful talk with other friends. As I grow more familiar with the university I am continually discovering men I knew in similar conditions on earth. Sometimes we laugh together over the surprisingly mundane form taken by our 'Crowns, white robes and harps'. Needless to say, we are heartily glad that the reality is otherwise and that we are able to follow our natural bent and enjoy the kind of life most suited to us. There is Dr. G, for instance, with his shortsighted eyes and kindly face whose whole world, as I remember him, was contained within the walls of his college. Here he is, no longer short-sighted or stooping but still working at the same task with vigour and understanding. He said to me: 'My dear fellow, I naturally gravitated here because this is the only kind of life I understand or care for, but I know well that I am making a mistake. Unless I want seriously to stunt my growth I shall have to dig myself out of here and try some other kind of life.'

I demurred, thinking of his great value as a teacher
and leader of youth but he tells me he has reached a
stage in self-knowledge where he cannot deny the
necessity to move on and that I shall find that it comes
to us all sooner or later.

'The timelessness of our life,' he said, 'misleads us
into thinking that there is no longer any period to our
happiness. We have no lengthening shadow of old age
to put a natural limit to our activities and so when
we are happy and easy we think it can continue indefinitely. But I know there are natural periods in our
time here and that I am approaching one of them. I
could perhaps disregard the intimations and stay on
here, but if I did so I should be perverting the pattern.
So you see that even paradise may not be enjoyed for
too long lest it thwart one's proper growth.'

This seemed to me a hard saying and I was not sure
that I understood then the full import of his words.
Even as he spoke, however, the illumination of his
wise spirit made a glory all around him and was more
convincing than many words. I hesitated, but took
courage to say to him: 'When you speak of a change
you feel coming, are you anticipating a change in
yourself or just a change of place and occupation?'

'It will, I think and hope, be both,' he answered. 'I
am growing old in this body and shall soon be done
with it. Then I shall go on to explore this wonderful
universe on another level.'

'This then, is the kind of "second death" I have
heard of?' I asked.

'Yes, you can call it that, certainly,' he said, 'but I

have no knowledge of when this may happen so we will say no more about it. I have loved this place and these people and it will be hard to leave them, but no real parting is involved because I shall keep in touch.'

I had heard of this second death and transition to the next sphere but my own development is as yet so imperfect that I had not given it any serious thought. Now it seems that I may be privileged to watch it happening to another. Coming and going between ourselves and a higher world is possible to a limited degree and I knew that Dr. G. would keep his word. This interchange tends to be a one-way traffic, because although the higher can come back to the lower at the cost of some deprivation of light and speed of being, the lower cannot easily bear the higher conditions until those changes in the bodily make-up occur to which Dr. G. referred. Death bears an aspect of doom while one is on earth and cannot see beyond it, but now one can see that death is a simple change of condition necessary for growth. As our present body fulfils its purpose and is outworn the succeeding and more glorious form glows through it and a gradual metamorphosis begins which finishes in a period of unconsciousness and an awakening in a higher sphere. I am intensely interested in this change and have asked Dr. G. to allow me to follow it as closely as possible. When I made this request he looked at me with some doubt; my proposal savoured of impertinence and I hastily apologised and withdrew it. But he has reassured me and has asked me to come and meet his closer friends. This I have done and have been welcomed to a choice inner circle of men and women all of whom find in Dr. G. a quality as leader and guide and who also love him as a man.

Parting is not spoken of among us. We know that in its more human and earthly sense it has no meaning for us. There is no sadness, only a subdued joy in the lovely changes we see unfolding in our friend. He is continuing his usual work with his students and is always available to his friends but we watch the progressive concentration of his life into a glowing interior brightness. It is as though the light and warmth that normally flow out from him to bless his friends is being withdrawn and collected within so that this illumination burns through and is wasting away his outer lineaments.

The end came suddenly. I called on him and was told that he was sleeping. We stood around and watched his still form and the light which waxed and waned there. In a breathtaking second the change came. The light gathered itself together and burnt itself to a keen *thought* of light so intense and inward that we gasped and turned aside. Then it had gone and only a wraith of our friend remained which shrank away and disappeared as we watched.

We sat speechless, absorbed in the beauty and meaning of the transition. It was long before anyone broke the silence and then one said: 'I have heard that some time is needed for a spirit to get used to the new conditions, just as we needed time to adjust when we

first came here, so we must not expect our friend to
come to us yet. I suggest that when an interval has
elapsed we should meet here again and wait and hope
for his coming.' We agreed to this and went off full of
thought to our various occupations.


Book producing remains a joy and satisfaction to me
and I am going on learning and making, but I want
also to write – another urge I never fully satisfied on
earth. I do not count this as writing; this has to be a
process of creation at second hand and it is severely
restricted by the limitations of the hand and brain of
the transmitting medium. Also it has to conform to
the powers of understanding of those who may read it
and who have not as yet attained to the experiences it
recounts; this means that the special powers and in-
sights of this plane of being cannot be fully employed.
In common honesty this has to be a factual account
and so gives me no licence to create. No, I am longing
to do some original work inspired by the wonder of
the world as I now know it, and so I have gone back
to my cottage and left for a time the cheerful companionship of the university. Ingram knows of my
design and approves of it. So I am trying to express
something of the splendour and awe of my experience
in this marvellous phase of existence. World on world
of ascending being are opening up to me in vision and
by intuitive knowledge and the impulse to add to the
human comment on their infinite vistas is not to be
denied.

I am living in a withdrawn dream of timelessness and wonder and am well content to try to transmit its openings of beauty and awe. It is impossible to follow such experiences in earth terms so I forbear the effort. My travail is resulting in a scanty output of what I hope is poetry. I cannot be sanguine about its worth but I am content that I have faithfully striven.

I am back in the university and it is good to rejoin my friends. They have respected my desire for solitude and have refrained from even the interference of thought. I have shown my effort to Thomas who gives a modified approval and has decided that I may print it. So I am busying myself with types and format and shall produce a book of my own at last.

As I work my thought has been going back over my life since that far-off day when earth closed for me. I can see now that all this while I have been half-consciously trying to complete my earth experience; to fill in its gaps and make good some of its deficiencies. I know, and Mitchell has warned me of it, that the great lack for which I can never now compensate is my failure to accept the ordinary human responsibilities of marriage and parenthood. I have pondered much over this particular lack. I suppose that an overblown egotism and fear of failure operated to paralyse my power to love or to risk all in human relationship, much less to make myself responsible for other lives on earth. I do not know whether I have made it clear that the discipline of this life has brought all these weaknesses and mistakes by degrees up into full consciousness. I am now very alive to the defensive egoism which spoilt and wasted my years on earth. Now by the clearer vision born of suffering I am being set free from this self-imposed imprisonment. It is becoming easier to allow myself to flow out in freedom to others and to take what they offer without constraint. But nothing can compensate fully for what I have missed; nothing here can parallel the all-and-everything condition of close human relationships on earth. Nevertheless I wish if possible to make some belated gesture of confidence in fate and willingness to pledge my freedom to another. A stern struggle with my self-centred ego has resulted in a visit to Mitchell to whom I have opened my difficulty.

Mitchell smiled at me with that warmly human affection of his which always shames my cool detachment.

'Your instinct is right and wise,' he said, 'but think well before you go on. For yourself, this may be the right course, but notice how your egoism has trapped you even here inasmuch as you have not considered how your present attitude would affect any woman with whom you tried to establish a lengthy connection. Will she, when she realises your motive, appreciate being used as compensation for an experience of which you wilfully deprived yourself on earth? Don't you see that if this project is to work it must grow out of your real need for a particular woman and her need of you as her particular man?'

I was abashed at this revelation of ingrained self-regard and lack of understanding. How much I have still to learn about my abominable self and its shameless habits! I assured Mitchell that I would be patient and wait to find the woman who would perhaps value me and whom I could value apart from any use we might have for each other in terms of development. After my flights into the zenith of poetic fervour and consequent over-blown ego, this dose of humility brings me back to my proper level. Mitchell does me good as always with his robust common sense and the free-flowing affection he gives to each and all of us who pass through his hands. When human problems are in question there is no more reliable guide. The work he does in conditioning and helping newcomers to find their feet in this novel and sometimes bewildering world is invaluable. So I am back in the university humbled, but hopeful and content to wait and let life teach me by actual contacts with men and women some of the lessons I failed so lamentably to learn on earth.

# Chapter 7

## PURGATION

DR. G. HAS kept his promise to come to us but he appeared when we were least expecting him. Some few of us were sitting quietly talking when his voice suddenly took up the parable and as we looked up, startled, we saw the outlines of a form which speedily filled in and took substance and there he was among us again. He brought with him an exalted air and we felt his presence as a spiritual baptism, a stream of pure joy absorbed hungrily by our thirsty beings. Light and happiness glowed up in us too with the pleasure of heightened being. He stayed only a short time, made a characteristic remark about the 'sordid fug' in which we chose to live and left us again. We knew how to interpret this; his finer being could only with difficulty tolerate our conditions and to try to detain him would have been unkind. However, we resolved that next time we would make better use of the opportunity and we prepared certain questions so that we might put them to him without loss of time.

Then I had a better idea. Why not get him to answer our questions by the 'absent' method so that when he made his rare personal appearances we were free just to enjoy his actual presence? The inspiration of this had stilled all mental activity before and had made us mere receptors of his wonderful influence. We decided to try the other method and later some of us got together and were able to find him and to talk to him for long spells at a time.

As to the questions we put to him, they were at first mainly to do with the conditions of his new life and he did his best to describe them to us. He had the same difficulty in conveying the differences to us as I have in making our conditions clear to an earth intelligence. In the transition from plane to plane alterations in the scope of consciousness produce baffling changes in the very framework of thought; categories of space and time are radically modified so that to an unchanged consciousness, more limited in its scope, these are almost incommunicable. His world was like ours, he said, but matter was more fluid and more easily influenced by thought. Here on this plane, as I have said before, a desire to find any person or place sets one's feet moving in the right direction; there, Dr. G. told us, transit is swifter and more independent of the time-space factor. One's movement is almost simul-

taneous with one's thought so that to desire to be with
friends is to find oneself among them. The speed with
which thought is translated into act and the lessening
of material hindrances to desire is all part of the increased tempo of living and since one's body is now
far lighter and more responsive, such a speed of living
feels right and natural to it.

Language is less used and thought and feeling are
directly and fully apprehended. Ease in all the processes of living speeds up its rate so that even the
swiftness of exchange among us is to him tedious and
sluggish. Light, the concomitant of life and an index
of its speed and intensity is far more keen and pure.
Colour, he tells us, is less to be seen by the eye, but its
essence is piercingly known by the spirit. So with all
the joys of sense; they are there in a purity of essence
which makes all our slower, more outward enjoyment
like a vague dream. We got here a swift glimpse of an
entirely different way of sensing one's world: by a
direct and immediate spiritual awareness of its
spiritual qualities.

This and much more he told us, not to make us dis-
contented with our present lot, but to open our eyes to
the inner truth of what actually exists in our present
experiences waiting to be born in purer form as soon
as we are ready to bear it. Since Dr. G. left us, we
have talked among ourselves of the metamorphosis to
which we are coming, but we are honest enough to
recognise our present unfitness. Our happiness here is
for most of us as great as we are able to bear, and far
from being satiated with it in its present form, we are

only too content for it to continue. Moreover, should a man try to live in that rarified spiritual air who carried still in his being the uncleansed stains of earth his sufferings would be terrible, as intense as the joy of which he would be capable when he is cleansed of them. In other words, with the increased powers of living and enjoying would go an increased sensibility to suffering which would make any guilt or remorse intolerable in its intensity. We admit our unreadiness; most of us still have Christian's burden on our backs in the shape of sins and weaknesses we have yet to deal with. I myself am conscious of a despairing load, far more, it seems to me now, than I could possibly have realised on earth. What were merely venial and even permitted errors and cruelties on earth look far blacker to me now. As one's understanding grows, the import of actions and motives becomes clearer, self-deception is less possible and the clearer one becomes the blacker becomes one's view of the past. Yet I have had to revise this attitude of mind as I shall tell.

I suppose the great task we have before us in this stage of being is to free ourselves from a sense of guilt, notwithstanding our clearer view of the harm our wrongdoing has occasioned. One cannot just lay down the burden with a sigh of relief and go on free of it. Burden is an inadequate metaphor; the mischief is in us, a dark cloud at the heart of our emotional being. It is a disease that has to be cured. Seeing it in these physical terms makes it plain that the old idea that sin can be paid for by another is an illusion. We each have to wrestle with our own mortal illness until we can achieve a cure. I am attempting to understand my own case; all I know is that the smart and shame of wrongdoing make a hard core of unease at the heart of living. I am aware of some amelioration of my state from time to time but complete cure is yet a long way off. Mitchell counsels patience and assures me that the healing process will go on perhaps the better if I can cease to brood over it and give myself more fully to the life around me. I know this to be good advice and am following it with varying degrees of success.

Now – and this makes me wonder whether those who advocate a complete break with earth are not right – I have heard that a disquieting disclosure which concerns my family has become public and this touches me deeply. I know that but for the spotlight of fame this would have remained buried in a decent mediocrity which invites no question. Fame! I am trying to be honest about it now. I intended to be famous and I saw the situation in the East during the First World-War as being made for exploitation by my ambition. I did exploit it too, in every subtle and hidden way that opened; watched it for my own advantage and worked and planned for my opportunity. I buried all this in an unquiet conscience. True, I loved my country and wished to serve her, but I knew that I sinned in every life I sacrificed to my ambition. In the upshot many lives paid for my success and perhaps years of enduring mischief, even to those I most wished to benefit, came from the hopes I raised and failed to satisfy. This failure had always tasted to me like treachery and it poisoned all my achievement. It

poisoned all my ensuing life on earth and now I have
to know that the aftermath of fame is injuring those I
loved.

I felt at first that I could never reach the depths of
humility where I should be able to carry this Judas-
load. I knew myself as no fit company for my friends
so I have left the university to seek counsel of Mitchell
and to try what the solitude of my cottage can do for
me. Mitchell said: 'See, Scott, there *is* a solution;
one has got to adjust to what one is and forget what
one has wished others to think one is. One has to get
down to it and accept one's being on this lower level
and patiently and cheerfully start again. Go back to
your early days; try to realise how you built up the
legend of yourself and then began to live up to it. Try
to find the real man behind this façade and then the
source of your failure will become plain to you. I think
you already know it.'

His words flicked my raw humiliation and I have
left him for my cottage where I am spending a time of
intensive thought. He is right, of course; I have to
retrace my steps to the beginning of the legend and
find and accept the real person obscured by it. I am
tired of the wearisome weakness of lamenting over
failure and guilt. Mitchell said: 'Remember, there is
no blame; there is only cause and effect,' and I am
pondering that. Is all this self-blame a perverted form
of conceit? It is certain that no one can carry the full
load of responsibility for all the results of his deeds on
earth. This and that I did wrong, I misjudged, I was
blind, I was harsh and unjust. All these things are

continuing to fructify after their kind in earth affairs. I can no longer influence these effects; even if I were still on earth I could not alter the pattern. So what I have to face here and now is threefold: first, my knowledge of the evil I did; then my knowledge of its continuing effects on earth; and lastly, my knowledge of what it has made me, the visible and tangible evidences of which I bear about in my present bodily form.

I begin to feel that my present dilemma is only to be resolved rightly in the light of the legacies of my past lives. Re-incarnation assures me, in relation to the first two of my difficulties, that I shall meet again those who have been injured by my deeds in a future which will itself contain modifications due to my interference with the pattern, so that in two ways I shall again come to grips with my own evil and be given another chance to wrestle with it. The third result, the inescapable marks of my own deeds I bear in my own body, I am mercifully given time and opportunity here to cleanse and clear.

If one has borne even a small part in public affairs the results of mistakes and sins are public too. Normally, knowledge of earth happenings, even those touching one's own name and fame are hidden from us, and perhaps wisely so. Yet I have chosen to know and I have to balance against the dismay and suffering the pleasures of satisfied vanity when fame is kind. Mitchell says that the disproportion in seeming effects is an illusion; that to have been in the public eye does not mean that one's deeds, if evil, are any more heinous than those a private individual may commit although they may appear to affect a smaller circle of lives. In fact, large or small are impossible to determine on our scale of measurement and only the vanity of making some stir in the world makes us regard either sins or virtues as more important than those of other people. I need courage to face all this squarely; I am perforce learning a painful humility out of which a kind of fortitude seems to blossom. It may well be, as Mitchell says, that self-blame is really only my vanity tripping me up again, so no more of it.

The outcome of this searching experience is a conviction of the importance of the theory of re-incarnation. I need to know more about the law of Karma; how it operates and how far it may be responsible for the changes and chances of life on earth. Not that any such knowledge will exonerate me from full responsibility; it will only spread it over many more lives, since it seems that each succeeding life presents the same kind of problems and offers fresh opportunities to solve them.

Why should one sorrow over mistakes and wasted opportunities when each of us comes here eventually where conditions are kind and congenial? This diary of mine should supply an answer to that question. 'As a man sows, so also shall he reap' is true through every change that the human spirit can undergo. There can be no place left in an illimitable universe where it does not hold good. Yet there is still a reason for stressing the importance of the earth experience. It seems that in the cycle of growth this is the formative stage when alone any real growth in essence takes place. When the earth life is over and one comes here, the law of affinity takes one into congenial conditions and the general alleviation of circumstances removes all outer sources of conflict. There is no more struggle for existence. Our work here is a kind of mopping-up operation. We can, in fact we must, graduate from regions where our faults of temper and our sense of guilt are tolerated to those where we have to clear ourselves of these stains of earth. But although we may clear ourselves and in the ascent of the planes gradually purify our being until we are again essential spirit, still no actual growth in this spirit will have been made here. What we bring from earth remains our all, so our fate is bound up with our earth experiences; only in the struggle and turmoil of life there are we able to make any real difference to our spiritual stature. So, although this in-between period is a wonderful interlude, the real work has to be done on earth.

When the time comes for us to graduate from this sphere I am told that we may then be able to recall our past lives. That day will not dawn for me yet for I know that I need to be far more clear from my earth experiences before I shall be fit to face and assimilate this deeper knowledge of myself. I have still so many problems to get into focus that a more extended view of the scale of creation and the age-long process by which man creates himself as well as his world is becoming a necessity for me. I can at least get the general outline of the process clear in my mind, so let me try to set it out.

It must be something like this: primitive man when he first appeared on the earth in a recognisable human form probably lived a struggling and very brief existence there. Call this his first life-cycle – Life A. He dies, and finds himself here in these planes. Probably he is unable to progress far and so returns rather quickly to begin cycle B. Now he is a more complex being and his essence is a compound of both these lives so Life B should really be shown as B a. Again the process is repeated and he returns to earth for Cycle C as a composite being, C b a. In each return here after death on earth the man will tend to make higher progress and to spend longer away from earth since his essential spirit is being steadily enriched by earth experience and each time he returns to earth he will be a richer and more composite personality.

Since he bears in himself, not the *memories* of his past lives, but the tendencies they have built into his being, his earth lives will be likely to show a typical pattern; he will tend to come up against the same order of problems and crises of fate in life after life even though each life may be set in a different era of world history and maybe in different countries or races. Yet his own particular pattern of response to environment and circumstance will recur unless and until he overcomes the weaknesses which invite it. While he continues to fail his tests, in fact, they will continue to recur.

I have heard of a man who in life after life has been killed in battle during his youth. Never once has he

been able to behave in such a way as to escape this
fate. He has never known old age, nor will he do so
until he can recognise and control the aggressive impulse at the moment of crisis and so conquer his fate.
Then the pattern will take a different form and will be
modified for good. Then he will be able to finish his
course and to learn the lessons of maturity which up
to now he has missed. This is an extreme example,
but the karmic law it illustrates may explain many of
the queer twists of fate and the otherwise inexplicable
tragedies which do overtake men.

Another outcome of karma is the way in which
each earth life recapitulates the pattern of those which
have gone before in series as they originally occurred.
If one thinks of it, one has always known that the
embryo re-enacts every stage in human evolution and
that birth takes place only when the fully human stage
is reached. It now seems that re-capitulation goes on
after birth as well, the pre-conscious lives being repeated during the early stages of infancy and later
lives influencing the adolescent and the young man or
woman. For instance, the phenomenal rate of growth
of the head during early childhood may well be a re-
capitulation of a period of swift mental development
during the early human phase. Later in life one can
often observe sharply marked stages in the lives of
men, sudden and unpredictable swervings aside from
previous habits of life and behaviour, shown in
changes of occupation and almost of temperament as
each past life makes its influence felt. What a study
is here! No wonder that we spend so much time in

our universities piecing together the evidence and trying to understand something of the wonderful processes at work.

The history of man on the earth has not been long enough for any of us to have made many appearances during historical times, although the immense ages during which man was climbing from an unconscious level to a conscious state of being must have seen continual rebirths at very short intervals. Suppose a man to have got to his eighth cycle; he will come back to earth for cycle H and this life will be modified by all the previous ones so that it should be shown as Life H *gfedcba*. He will thus have seven re-capitulations to work through before he embarks on the contemporary lifetime and the lifework proper of Lifetime H. He will have the combined tendencies of these seven previous lives as an enrichment of his present personality; he will have a strongly reinforced personality, perhaps one with many twisted and difficult problems awaiting the opportunities of a new life for their solution, perhaps a matured and enriched personality if his problems have been attacked with courage in a previous lifetime. Whatever he has made of the challenges of each lifetime will remain to him as strength or weakness in facing the tasks of the present one. It is certain that the challenges he has failed to meet and overcome will present themselves again in Life H in a modern form, and if again he fails the pattern will go on unaltered so that they will meet and challenge him again in the succeeding life. What we must take into account is the progressive complication of the life-pattern, its enrichment and added subtlety and above all, the mercy which never allows failure to be final and irrevocable. Karmic debts are only cancelled as we gain the grace and strength to cancel them ourselves, but the opportunity to do so comes to us in this inevitable repetition.

Pondering deeply on all this, seeing in my mind's eye the long pageant of a man's progress, watching him as he raises himself out of the mire of earth and losing sight of him as he transcends sphere after sphere and is finally lost to sight in the formless splendour of eternity the paradox of that periodic descent into matter and time of a spiritual and timeless entity is forced on the understanding. Here we reach a mystery —the return of the timeless into the stream of time, of the immaterial into the prison of matter. There is only one way of thinking of it; the mystery of this descent into matter and time is only revealed in the living of it.

The sense of duration, which is each individual's measure of passing time, is checked and regulated on earth by exterior standards set according to earth movements and position with regard to the sun, hence time is a highly formalised concept which over-rides the individual sense of duration. Here the exterior checks are absent and we begin to realise that our sense of duration is a function of our kind of consciousness and alters as the scope of that consciousness widens. In other words, the rate of experiencing quickens as we ascend and so the change over from time to timelessness comes about gradually as we are fitted to adjust to it. My experience here has already shown me the beginning of this gradation. Up to the present – and you must remember that I have not yet progressed far – I have reached a stage of consciousness where I am aware of a great difference between my rate of living and the tempo of all my activities and those of men still on earth. Granted that men vary in their tempo even on earth, but taking one's experience in working with a medium as a guide, I find that I can only with difficulty slow down my rate to work with a mind still subject to earth conditions. It is tedious and fatiguing and sometimes I think nearly impossible, but it can just be done. At a higher stage I imagine that a word for word communication would become impracticable and there would have to be just a swift interchange of thought.

But to return to the point which, because it is the heart of the mystery, fascinates me: how are we to think of the translation back into time of the spirit, which is a timeless principle of the being, when it has to return again into a body and become subject to time? This is the crux of the mystery. I can only suppose that when the final stage of purification is reached and the false limits of the ego have faded out so that essential, de-limited spirit alone remains, it is drawn back in simplicity and obedience to fate into the stream of living, there to learn, suffer and enjoy and grow in the space-time strait-jacket of earthly conditions.

Now, how does all this help me with my special problems? It corrects my sense of proportion and puts

the events of one lifetime into their place as parts of a
sequence in which they have only a long-term significance. What that is, I shall only understand fully when
I can see the whole and for this comprehensive vision I
am not yet fitted. But it does more for me than that:
I am made to know that there will come a time when I
shall be given another opportunity to deal with my
problems, to pay my debts and I hope, to avoid in-
curring a further weight of guilt. So to understanding
succeeds hope. Then Mitchell tells me that when the
sequence of the past unrolls for me there will be much
good in it as well as error and failure and that by then
I shall be able to balance these things with an equal
fortitude, without elation over the one or despair over
the other. Already, thinking over my particular mistakes in the light of the long record of the past and
seeing myself standing here as it were midway between
that past and a future stretching ahead into the light
of other ages, I am conscious of relief, of the peace
of acceptance, and of the sloughing off of the intolerable burden of my earth persona and the legend I
fostered and lived by.

There is another aspect of rebirth which I have only
just come to understand. We come here after death in
a form very like that of earth and it perpetuates the
faults and failures of our earth bodies. A cripple, for
instance, will come here with a defective body and
although the defect will be modified he will remain
recognisably the same person, neither beautifully
angelic if he has been puny and ugly nor an athlete
if he has been an ailing invalid. Bodily conditions

matter less and less of course as development of the spirit goes on, but the same essential form is kept throughout because in a subtle way bodily form does condition emotional and spiritual form.

You might therefore think that those who happen to be born in a handsome and virile body have an undue advantage; up to a point this is true although many such are handicapped by the vanity engendered by their lovely physical appearance and are by no means so good to look at in their astral forms. But the framework of beauty is there and when the faults that mar the being are corrected it shines out again in surpassing loveliness. But whatever form one starts with, in the ascent of the planes the appearance, good or bad, is gradually superseded and finally form is lost in light; but this is to speak of the very end of a long journey and on the way the disabilities of a poor form may still have to be borne.

Rebirth provides us all with a fresh start, with a body differently conceived and developed and the connection between what has been made of the previous life and this new form is likely to be a closely causative one. The poor cripple who has courageously surmounted his disability and transmuted it into spiritual strength and beauty may now be clothed with a body of beauty and strength; the handsome man may well find himself inhabiting a poorer form if his spiritual being has been impoverished by vanity and selfishness. In his next embodiment he may have to learn the lessons of weakness and ugliness. But in any case each of us will escape from the prison of our present form and begin a new cycle with a different physical equipment.

It is thought here, and I think so too, that a change of sex is probably made at intervals. After all, men and women are the two sides of creation and experience of one sex only would leave a sadly one-sided and impoverished being. We need to know by experience how the other side of creation lives and to add the strengths and skills of woman to man, of man to woman. When the proper time comes the change is made, and this is not merely a matter of theory. Those who can testify to their past lives are witnesses to this change and I have come across several instances of it. I have talked this aspect of rebirth over with Mitchell and he is emphatic about it. We have spoken of the way in which recapitulation of the themes of a past life acts as a kind of fate in the destiny of a man. The reversal of sex can sometimes be a powerful agent in altering the pattern of a life and giving a man the chance to break a sinister sequence of events which, without this change, may again prove too strong for him. For instance, Mitchell himself has been several times a man but it seems clear to him that his pattern of life will not be corrected without the interposition of a woman's experience on his next descent to earth. He it was who has never lived past his youthful years on earth but again and again has been drawn into conflict and has fallen in battle during his youth. He feels that if he is again given the form of a man the same fate my recur, the same chivalrous and aggressive impulse will betray him into the same action. To combat his particular temptation he may need to live in a form where the temptation is lessened and thus be able to break the recurring pattern for good.

Whether a change of sex is involved or not, the taking of a new form is a necessary condition of new experiences and it must radically modify and enrich the being so that it may adventure freely into new paths. In all these thoughts about rebirth one is reassured by the extraordinary rightness of the provisions it makes for the growth of the essential being. I find it hard not to credit a clearly divine plan of which we here get a glimpse. True, natural processes in their promotion of growth are always a marvel of adaptation of means to ends; as one studies them on earth it is easy to put the cart before the horse and say that the growth and adaptation come about only by the mechanical operation of the stresses and strains provided by the environment, but here we have additional evidence and can see beyond that argument because for us the element of strain in the environment is relaxed and yet the evidence for a planned development is stronger.

I can see so clearly that in the ideal conditions of our 'heaven' only a process of purification of what has already been formed on earth takes place. Yet I think we all know of a certainty that the purpose of the universe is that every entity should grow into the perfection of its own type. So I for one see clearly and accept the necessity for yet other earth experiences in other and perhaps stranger forms and in succeeding aeons of earth time so that this great end may be finally achieved in me. What is the end? Here we trespass on a province of eternity; it makes no sense to speak of an end to what is of infinity.

# Chapter 8

FRIENDS AND ASSOCIATES

I WANT NOW to speak of some of my friends here because during my own critical personal experiences I have still lived a life among men and have been well-befriended.

Since I found the university and became free of its courts my life has alternated between active work with Thomas on book production, occasional spells of more academic work and times when I have savoured the luxury of solitude in my cottage. This has made for me a well-balanced life, harmonising the main trends of my nature. There is no coercion here and no tyranny of time so when one kind of life palls one can freely exchange it for another. There is a constant coming and going at the university and study, recreation and fellowship all play their parts in its life, but students frequently go off for spells of other kinds of experience and return when they are ready.

The salt of existence here as on earth is the fellowship of one's peers and I have been singularly fortunate in finding kindred spirits among widely differing types of men, for although segregation into planes produces a harmony of development, this does not imply a monotony of types.

Thomas I have spoken of before. He has been a quiet and undemanding background to my university life and whatever the project on hand I have looked around to make sure that he was by my side. He is far from being a mere yes-man and often administers salutary criticism; he thinks nothing of my fits of feverish activity and if he judges the results poor will calmly destroy the lot however much I may rage. I am always the amateur and he the professional who knows and as, of course, I really concur in this classification we work together in a give-and-take of slightly uneasy harmony which I like far better than an uneventful calm. He has a weight and steadiness which balance my fervour and his quiet reasonableness is for me a touchstone of sense. As we work together there is a quiet glow of contented affection and shared interest which, when on occasion we differ, sends out sparks of amicable conflict and occasionally flares out in gusts of uncontrollable laughter when my irreverent tongue triggers off some absurdity that even Thomas cannot take seriously.

I owe a great deal to Thomas. At times when my

own conflicts have reduced me to despair a spell of
work with him who, for my sake, will tolerate the
sultry conditions I create, often restores me to normal
again. He tells me that he used to be a clerk in a
printing house and always had longed to take a more
effective part in the production of books, but a defective education and consequent lack of opportunity
denied him advancement. He had married, and on his
small salary had brought up two daughters. His wife
pre-deceased him and he had struggled on alone until
the girls were launched; then on a fine spring morning
his foot slipped and an oncoming bus crushed out his
life. All this happened at much the same time as my
own passing but I had to work through the uneasy
experiences of my early days here before our paths
converged. His wife, he told me, had never been very
closely knit to him and when he found her again she
had formed other ties in which she was well content
so he felt himself free to follow the work he had
always wanted to do and now did so well. At the
same time he was able to take advantage of the better
education offered by the university. How very much
of the joy of our lives here consists in this freedom to
overpass the frustrations of earth! Whatever Thomas
touches he grasps quietly and sanely. His considerable
mental power is exerted with a steady enjoyment and
as a craftsman he has genius. I am proud to call him
friend and comrade.

Of late, I have noticed an uncharacteristic restlessness in him and it seems likely that his warmly affec-
tionate nature is beginning to feel the need for a mate

and companion. I do not think his search will be a long one; there is a certain damsel of this college with an irrepressible gaiety of spirit who yet seems to be attracted by his warm and solid worth.

A friend who has made an unexpected appearance in my life is a young man named Edgar R. who came here a very long time ago. His story is a sad one and explains the length of time he has needed in this plane. Is it horrifying to know that he was a murderer? In a moment of frenzy he killed his wife and the law then sent him to death with all the usual accompaniments of shame and violence. I can well imagine the impossible conditions into which at first he drifted. His own shame and despair drew him to the darkest regions of the early planes and his plight there was awful. He hid himself among the debased and brutal population of a town of ill-repute, afraid that his victim would find and reproach him. Here he lived in a dark hell of his own making, a prey to fear and remorse. There are certain devoted souls who manage to penetrate to these regions in search of any who can be helped and they found Edgar eventually and persuaded him to face his problem, come out of hiding and find his wife.

She also had suffered. Anger and hatred of him had prevented her progress, but by degrees she was helped to see and understand the real situation for which she had been partly responsible, but which had been hidden from her by the mists of her own anger. These two poor souls were still bound to each other by wrong-doing which seems to make nearly as strong a

bond as love itself. Until they had cleared the anger
from their souls and the blindness from their eyes they
could not get free. They neither of them wished to
remain together, or so they thought at first; yet when,
by the help of those who are skilled in bringing about
such adjustments they did at last face the evil in themselves instead of condemning it in each other, the
change in their whole condition produced a strange
solution. They each laid hold again upon their essential innocence; they renewed the long-lost appearance
of youth and charm and to their own surprise they
found that the bond which really held them together
was love.

They are together now in an ideal relationship and
the joy they take in each other has been won through
long purgatorial suffering. So the clumsy bungling of
human justice has been compensated by the justice of
God. This is not the sentimental notion of mere for-
giveness of sins – that would alter nothing – but a true
regeneration through suffering and the cleansing of
the perilous stuff which would otherwise continue to
poison the springs of living. Although I know of the
black spots in this world where there seems to settle
an irredeemable silt of the base and brutal, I am convinced by many such tales of rescue and redemption
that ultimately all of these unfortunates will make
their way up into the sunshine and will there work out
their own salvation. Edgar then, and his charming
wife are happy and useful members of our community
and when the time comes it looks as though they may
be ready to go on together.

Another man who has come into our circle lately is the man of great potential value whom Mitchell found in very bad case and quite lost in a dangerous region and for whom he asked my help. I am interested because his case was a little like my own and because Mitchell had asked my help so I followed Tom Harris' course with special concern. With his potentialities for greatness he had yet been unable to rise above his humble beginnings on earth and the continual frusttration of his will to power had made him bitter and anti-social. He had finally been driven into the false attitude where evil had become his good and his many gifts had been prostituted to the service of a contempt and hatred of the ordinary run of mankind. Two things only had kept his soul alive: he had retained an enduring love of beautiful music and he had one great devotion to a woman who had been able to penetrate the unlovely shell of him to the nobility within. But here he was, seething with black hatred and scorn of his fellows and all his strong and generous nature poisoned at its source.

Tom Harris could not be brought straight into what we call Mitchell's clearing house but Mitchell was with him constantly for a while and several of us took a hand and tried to gain his confidence. Once he was really convinced that he could trust us and that he need not, and in fact, could not, despise us, the black cloud of his despair and hatred began to clear. At intervals he still blew up in the most alarming way and we had to stand clear until the cataclysm of his rage died down. We nicknamed him 'old Vesuvius' and the

title did not displease him at first. But he grew
pathetically anxious to be admitted to our fellowship
and as soon as the realisation dawned that the only
hindrance was in himself, Mitchell got a chance to
make him understand how things work here and what
are the conditions that necessarily govern all our relationships with each other. I remember that he nearly
annihilated us with rage when he was told that we
couldn't stand his smell; at that time it was really
enough to poison us all. But we managed to stand our
ground and by degrees he understood the difficulties
he made for himself and for us and then improvement
was rapid. He was beautiful when at last his magnifi-
cent body began to come clear and its stature became
apparent. His almost timid joy when he began to find
out how to use his great power beneficently was a
lovely thing to watch. He developed a great capacity
for gentleness, the real concomitant of strength which
somehow he had never found before.

We were all fascinated by Tom and by the speed
and almost spectacular nature of the changes in his
make-up. Mitchell said: 'Notice how this man was
feared and hated by his fellows and that it took a
woman's insight to find and love the potential greatness we are watching develop in him. She will have
much joy of him when she comes.' I think Mitchell
himself has great joy of Tom Vesuvius too. This rescue
work is his passion and when one understands the
hazards he runs to make these difficult contacts and
the hurts and injuries sustained by his body in brav-
ing the harmful emanations, one can better appreciate

the heroism of this work. I have known Mitchell fail when some desperate case has refused his help and drifted back into dark and misty regions where it is almost impossible to reach it. But I have never known him to give up and again and again he will go out and scout on the borderlands to bring in the stragglers, always hopeful that sooner or later the lost one will return within his range again. He is, of course, not the only one engaged in this sort of work; there are many other devoted souls able to penetrate the depths according to the toughness of their make-up and the consequent length of time they can safely stay down there. We all lend a hand on occasions but during the long period since Mitchell began this work he has had much experience and knows well how to inspire confidence and hope in the lost.

But to return to Tom Harris. He grieved terribly for his wife and her grief for him affected him strongly, although as usual she could not pierce the darkness of earth and know when he was present with her. Fortunately for his passionate and powerful nature there was no long waiting and the timing of her coming was perfect. Tom had almost cleared the dark cloud at the centre of his being and so could meet her in his true form and nature at last. So another story had a happy ending as I suppose all stories must have here. It is true that there can be great distress when a man and woman are united again here only to find their disaffinity and that their future course cannot run together. One may be unable to get beyond the early planes and the other may be for onward; although one can hold back voluntarily for awhile, sooner or later the second body must be discarded and the spirit released to go on farther. Many of the ties made on earth seem to be of this evanescent nature. Sentiment and loyalty keep people together for a time who have no real affinity but as soon as they are strong enough to face reality they can part happily and go on to find their real mates.

For me, now that I have become clearer and steadier, my search for a mate is in abeyance. The 'not-impossible-she' awaits me somewhere. Is she still on earth? Has she gone on before me? Shall I find her at all in this cycle or must I wait for long ages until I come again to earth? If she is here and within my range I shall find her, but it may be that the very fastidiousness which keeps me from casual relationships is an indication of her absence. Meanwhile I find joy, interest and satisfaction in the society of my friends of either sex and am content to wait until the turning wheel of existence brings her again within my ken.

I have had the joy of meeting again some of my friends and colleagues in the Services but of them it is not fitting to speak. One only I will mention because his coming illustrates a too-common problem. What happens to the unfortunate soul who puts an end to his own existence? In many – in most of such cases the pressure of work and worry, combined with private misfortune have unsettled the reason – or this is the would-be charitable verdict of the Coroner's Court. There are few men who have not in their make-up that weak point at which control breaks down. In most cases courage has been sapped by self-pity and so the breach is carried by a flood of despair. No man can judge, because each of us has his breaking point whether life tests us to the limit or not.

The friend of whom I speak was found almost immediately and I was able to go to him. He was in a kind of stupor and I was told that he might remain in this state for a long time and that nothing could be done about it. We watched over him and were loath to leave him in the misty half-region where he was found. It was a tract I myself had known in time past. Until he regained consciousness there he had to remain; had we forcibly removed him his poor body would not have been able to stand the conditions of our plane and so we had to leave him there. Now and again I went back to find him still in the same quiet coma, and seeing the state of his astral form I almost dreaded his awakening.

Suicides often show this long-lasting coma. It is really a merciful pause during which some of the damage to their emotional bodies is quietly made good. Much always remains for them to do when they come to themselves and in D – 's case, Mitchell asked me to make periodic visits to him so that he might find a familiar face when he awoke.

I made one such visit and found that he had gone. Knowing the agony of loneliness and 'lostness' one can suffer in this region of looming shadows I went immediately in search of him. I had only to let my feet take me swiftly in the direction of my strong desire

to find him and soon I made out his tall figure sway-
ing through the mist. I hailed him and he let me come
up but it was hard to make him see or hear me. In
fact, his body was so ill-developed that his new senses
were as yet of little use to him. By some means I got
him to come with me and led him into a slightly better
region and here he sank down and rested again. He
was reassured by his feeling of a friendly presence and
he has since told me that he recognised it as mine. So
he sunk again into sleep. I watched for some time and
then realised that he was deep under and might not
rouse again for a long time, so reluctantly I left him
there.

It would be tedious to describe the slow and uphill
progress he made. I was with him as often as possible
and as his senses developed and his body strengthened
I got him by degrees into better conditions. There was
much trouble to clear; remorse for his weakness, and
sorrow and fear all had to be cured. He is still unable
to join Mitchell in his 'home', but a delicate beauty
and grace is beginning to emerge and I am hopeful
of more rapid progress soon.

I am told that there is a belief that suicides remain
in coma until the time when they would normally have
died. This is one of those propositions which are impossible of proof, since no one can say when their hour
would have struck had they not anticipated it. It is a
fact that this state of coma lasts for varying periods,
but there is also a long period of unconsciousness in
many who have come by violent deaths. A suicide
differs from such a one because his emotional state is

usually far worse and takes much longer to clear, but a long period of coma may supervene on death in either case. Time is relative and the duration of unconsciousness to the sufferer is immaterial. Eventually he must awaken and take on the task of fitting himself to enter his own appropriate sphere of being. This is where he can be and is helped. There is often a long convalescence before he can get free of the sin and suffering of his violent end.

It is fitting that those who help him, pay their debt of sympathetic suffering, but we know the end, and it is glorious. There can be no such thing as final failure and this is where we have the advantage of earth. Even a relapse can be only temporary and there is never any occasion for despair, so I look forward with joy to the day when D – will be among us as a happy and fulfilled being with his mistakes and sorrows all behind him.

# Chapter 9

OUR WORLD AND ITS PEOPLE

IT MAY SEEM that I have gone fully into what happens to people, but have not provided them with a very solid earth to live on so I will try to repair the omission.

With the exception of the border regions of misty unreality, our earth is as solid and actual to our senses as the earth is to its denizens. The border lands are probably unreal largely because we come upon them before our new senses are functioning properly; to those who make their homes there no doubt they appear quite real. Once one's new senses have developed and are adjusted, this world has a solid surface with its physical features diversified as on earth and with a clothing of grass, trees and flowers. True,

these are of a finer texture and a more lucent beauty.
Again, much of the contrast with earth may be due to
our more ethereal senses but perhaps both the objective and subjective reality are different. I do not want
to paint a sentimental paradise but it is difficult to
avoid it. There is a serene unity about our conditions.
On earth you may go from the sordid hell of an in-
dustrial town to its clean and prosperous suburbs and
through these to the open country in a very short time,
but here the sordid hell is relegated to the lower planes
and populated by those who feel secure and at home in
such surroundings and the pleasanter types of country
are far removed from them. Thus in this region are
stately cities with all that an urbane town-dweller can
wish; noble buildings, churches, libraries and galleries
and all the amenities of civilisation for those who want
them. There are stretches of lovely country with parks
and mansions, wild regions of mountain and moor and
rivers and seas of incomparable beauty.

The necessity of producing and consuming food is
no longer a factor in our economy. Clothing and
luxuries are available freely for those who think they
want them, but greed so easily satisfied soon dies of
a surfeit. There are no extremes of temperature so
another spur to effort is missing. The fact that no one
*needs* food or any particular kind of clothing or hous-
ing removes the tension and fear from living altogether
and with this freedom a great deal of the element of
greed has vanished proving, if proof is needed, how
entirely greed is the child of fear and insecurity.

When people first arrive here the ease with which

any desired goods can be obtained sometimes goes to
their head and they begin to clutch and hoard as they
would have done on earth; but this is usually only a
temporary phase. If it is a deep-seated trouble they
probably gravitate to a lower plane where such attitudes can be tolerated but as a rule it is only a short-
lived madness. I could moralise a lot about the effects
of the removal of fear among us. In retrospect it is
easy to see how it plays the devil in human affairs and
is at the root of evils of various kinds. This is illus-
trated clearly by the effect of its absence. For what
have we to fear? We no longer fear death; it is a dis-
credited bogy. We no longer fear hunger nor thirst;
they do not exist. We no longer fear cold nor heat; our
climate is equable, or perhaps it would be more
accurate to say that our bodies do not register change
of temperature. There are no insurmountable barriers
of distance or difficulty; if we want to go to the ends
of the earth it is all open before us and our own desire
will guide us surely to any destination. With all these
material freedoms there is no frustration to engender
anger or bitterness, no fear to breed hostility, no
'haves' to cause envy and greed in the 'have-nots', and,
above all, no death to be feared as the ultimate evil.

In the old legend Satan was cast out of heaven but
allowed to work his will on earth. This reflects a necessary truth. There is no place for an evil principle here
and we have passed beyond the scope of nearly every
temptation. Here in the pure sunlight of happiness we
mature as we purge our bodies of their corroded ills,
but we can add nothing to our stature. That is to be

achieved, if at all by our lives on earth; all we can do here is to perfect what has been won there in the conflict. Here we simply consolidate our gains.

All this makes plain to me the necessity for the 'Adversary' in human affairs. It is only on earth that growth in the essential self takes place and this only through its conditions of strife and tension. Many wounds may be suffered and earth life may appear to show failure, humiliation and defeat. Yet these are a small price to pay for the actual gain in soul-stature. The wounds will be healed, the weaknesses strengthened and the sorrows of earth comforted here, since all such injuries are evanescent. The 'Judgement' is real enough, but it is not entirely concerned with the results of sinning and suffering. What is weighed is the growth of being which experience has produced. This is why the 'publican and sinner' go often into heaven before the 'good' man. So many of earth's solemn judgements are reversed or overturned here, where the scale of values runs in terms of being and not of behaviour.

I want now to explain how the various nationalities find their homes here. As might be expected there are replicas of each country here and men go to their appropriate national home, following naturally the law of affinity. You will find these replicas on each plane so that the vertical grading of society exists throughout. Thus each plane has inhabitants representing each nation and intervisitation on the same plane is easy and natural to us. Relations between national groups are friendly and a good deal of travelling and exchange of nationals goes on. The stupid barriers of language do not divide us to the same extent, since where words fail other ways of understanding are open to us and so no serious misunderstanding can arise. There appears to be less mingling of races on the lower planes where there does not seem to be the same desire to cross national boundaries. Among us, and still more so on higher planes, national distinctions become blurred and will finally be lost.

An interesting variation in our society is caused by the admixture of earth-ages as represented in any one plane. There can easily be people living in close harmony here together whose earth lives were separated by centuries, and this means that often the generations widely separated in earth time are simultaneous here. For instance, I may be associating with my grandfather, great-grandfather and so on for some generations back yet we shall all be roughly of the same age. The differences in our earthly experiences give rise to piquant interchanges and contrast and what I may call the 'living history' aspect of our society intrigues and delights the historian.

The structure of our society is therefore very diversified; it is stratified horizontally, as it were, and also vertically along the axis of time. Many people have been here for hundreds of years in earth time although they hardly ever realise this, and so one gets a mixture of the manners and customs of many ages and historical eras. There is certainly no danger of dullness because of a dead level of conformity; the bewildering variety of people, manners and outlooks is endlessly fascinating. While I have been associated with Mitchell it is understandable that most of my associates have been those recently arrived in these planes and most of them have been contemporaries of my own, or even from a later generation. The university too, tends to be filled with recent arrivals, but since I have become free of a wider society I am realising the possibilities of mixing with those of an earlier age.

I have a special friend who belonged to a knightly family in the middle ages. He went on crusade and eventually lost his life in Palestine. We have found much in common in our knowledge of and love for the Near-East. Glimpses of the real campaigns of those days that I get from his acounts are a wonderful corrective to the inaccurate romancing of the history books. His first-hand knowledge makes nonsense of the usual methods of research. His language also delights me. I found it hard to follow at first with its strong admixture of Norman-French, but when words fail us we can always get on by the exchange of thoughts. His interest in modern conditions and modern campaigns is as keen as mine in those of the past, so we are intensely pleased with each other's company. He is a simple soul whose creed of fighting loyally, feasting royally and thinking rarely or never has kept him in the lower planes for a long while where the fantasies of battle and feasting could continue. A gradual emancipation from these illusions freed him and he is learning now to adjust himself to a world where fighting is an anachronism but his restless energy often has to be worked off by long expeditions to the East. Imagine

visiting the desert in company with a fully armed
Crusader! He keeps the fashion of his clothing and
the accoutrements of his day, as most people do. Before long I shall ask his permission to accompany him
on his wild journeyings. I might even persuade him to
love the wild, free men of the desert as I do.

It is obvious that I have a great deal more exploring to do among those who, my contemporaries here
now, in measure of earth time were my predecessors.
So differently am I orientated since I got my own inner
tangles sorted out that social intercourse with all
manner of men is now my chief delight. It is very
seldom that the urge for solitude lays hold of me. My
friends on earth would find me altered; far more
blessedly ordinary, and free, thank God, from the
accursed legend which was for so long my prison.


I want now to try to deal with a subject of some difficulty. It may seem to certain people that, having made
sure of survival and of a state of blessedness partly
corresponding to the usual idea of heaven the need for
a religious belief and practice would either cease or be
very much modified. It is true that we survive but as
human beings still, not as angels, and until we become
angelic spirits the need for a religious background to
life is for most people as strong as ever. The naïve expectation that after death one comes straight into the
presence of one's Maker leaves out of account the im-
maturity and helplessness of the human spirit, and if
such a confrontation were possible one wonders

whether any created thing would survive the encounter. My own view of the situation is a limited one
and I can only record what I know from my own experience since I came here, experiences which do not
extend beyond the knowledge and outlook of the early
planes. I have mentioned the variety of types found
here; their bond of harmony is not in any uniformity
of temperament or outlook but in their having reached
a particular stage of development. In consequence of
this they are at home in the special atmosphere of this
plane. Granted this diversity of attitude one will expect
that religious views will vary just as much as on earth;
so they do, and there is provision here for every typical
attitude. Even the agnostic can maintain his position
because the Transcendent is still the Transcendent, and
the Absolute is still the Great Unknowable.

Habitual religious attitudes are of course modified
by our actual experiences. The process of purgation
through which we pass leaves the soul more free from
its strait jacket and more impelled to follow a path
which will lead finally to union with the Godhead.
Dogmatic teaching about heaven and hell is fortunately corrected by the known facts; freedom from the
cramping doctrines of eternal punishment, original sin
and predestination is a wonderful release for those
who have lived out their lives under such man-made
shadows. For the more philosophic, I suppose the great
discovery is that the whole scheme of things is built on
eternal justice and that any philosophy based on
materialism is untenable. It has to be seen as childish
and wilful ignorance which cannot be maintained here.

Immaterial and ignored aspects of our earth-bodies have here become solidly material and even this material is known to transmute again into the immaterial. In all this, study of our actual conditions and experiences must itself produce a re-orientation, a re-estimate of the real as against the transient and we have to admit that it is always the less material aspect which is the real and abiding, whereas the material is always the transient.

We know that our stay on any one plane is temporary and, however our estimate of time may compare with the earth calendar, this notion of progress from plane to plane as development justifies it is common knowledge here. There is room for much speculation and difference of opinion as to ultimate ends, of course. Much of the thought of higher spheres is open to those who care to know, but there are many here who are satisfied to enjoy the easy satisfactions of their care-free lives without speculating upon any further development. In general, I think that those who have farthest to go are most concerned with the journey. As I have said before, among thoughtful people at the university much study is given to the progress of the human spirit, its ascent of the planes and its probable return to earth when purification is complete.

But there is a vast multitude of good, well-meaning people here who are quite content to leave such problems to their pastors and teachers and for them some kind of church life is helpful and even necessary.

I watch all this with great interest. My own position is influenced by two factors – the mere logic of survival and of the conditions of life as I know it now and as I anticipate it in the further ranges of existence, and my researches into the minds and thoughts of those already in higher spheres. At least pessimism is dead and no negative attitude will stand up to the known facts. Whatever the chaotic thought of earth may achieve, we at least have the guarantee of experience for a lively faith in the love and eternal justice of the Absolute. This is a term I use in default of a better. I do not know if there may be lesser gods, advanced spiritual beings whose jurisdiction may have a more limited scope, but above and beyond all these I am convinced that the foundation and ground of all being must finally exist in the one Ineffable and Eternal Spirit.

# Chapter 10

## THE NEW VISION

THERE HAVE BEEN hints throughout this journal of the deep differences which develop here in one's ways of knowing external reality, but my difficulty in describing them, since I have no standard of comparison to which to appeal, is great. Earthly wisdom, I believe, has not got very far in analysing the process by which knowledge is obtained. I suppose if I had been asked when there, I should have made a tyro's effort and have said that knowledge originated in perception – seeing, hearing and feeling – and that this material was then worked upon by intellect to produce a reasoned scheme of things. No doubt many learned books of philosophy would be needed to give an adequate exposition of the process but since all earth-dwellers take it for granted in their daily experiences we can let it go at that. However it may be for earth, when I came here I soon found that my ways of apprehending and reasoning about things were very different.

Perception, in the early days here is very inadequate owing to the poor development of one's bodily senses. So one will expect that at first this world will have a misty and dreamlike quality. But as this condition clears, the kind of perception that takes its place is not of the same order as that on earth. It must not be forgotten that one's new body is emotional in its very nature and that therefore its new powers will be based on emotions. The total reaction to all that is seen or heard – the keener awareness, the swifter response, involves the whole emotional being. For instance, when I see a bush or a tree I am not able to perceive it simply in visual terms; I have to reckon on an emotional response to it. I like it, I value it, or even love it, or if I am not yet beyond a negative response I may dislike it or even hate it; but there will be a strong feeling reaction in either case. Similarly with one's reactions to people. They awaken the strongest response of all. A cool, detached, merely intellectual reaction to anything is practically impossible while we are in this emotional body. We have to see, hear and understand with our feelings and this gives a keener and more personal edge to all impressions. It is true to say that on this plane most of us are getting clear of emotional faults so that we do present a bewildering variety of beautiful forms and colours; hence the usual reaction to each other is that of appreciation and love. I think the nearest approach to our normal response is the spontaneous feeling of wonder, joy and almost worship which can be felt on earth when something utterly innocent and beautiful is seen and grasped by the emotions. This is the poet's vision, the artist's and perhaps the mystics too. In such a case, perception is not processed by the mind which is a cold and logical instrument, but impinges directly upon the feelings. Our approach to our world, then, can no longer be cold and impersonal.

I wish I could convey something of the flamelike lucidity of our process of reasoning. The emotional grasp of an impression is followed by an immediate awareness of the essential being of a thing and further thinking about it is a process of apprehending depth upon depth of meaning dwelling in the thing itself and in its relations with its environment. I cannot tell you how slow, formal and dead your processes of reasoning appear to us. In a flash we have made the whole journey to a conclusion which it may take you hours of painful thought to reach and which you will only cover in a superficial manner since what escapes in your reasoning is the precious element of meaning – significance. This for us becomes heightened to a degree I cannot convey in words. Wordsworth anticipated our method of seeing when he said that the meanest flower that blows could give him thoughts too deep for tears; in other words, the perception was felt directly upon the emotions. It is this power of ours to grasp depth upon depth of the richness of meaning inherent in everything, which, in retrospect, makes earth life look such a mean and poverty-stricken affair. If you can think of your most inspired moments – all too brief and infrequent in earthly experience – and imagine a life where this is the normal standard of living experience you will have a faint idea of what the future holds for you. It is obvious that the capacity to know, feel and understand in this scale of intensity has to be attained by degrees and that if it came before the cleansing process had at least been begun it would be too keen an agony to bear. Even then our scale of intensity is weak compared to that of the higher planes. I suppose, if you want to put it into pseudo-scientific terms you will explain it as world upon world, each of a higher system of vibration than its predecessor, but this really conveys very little. I want to put it in terms of actual living and this is not easy. Perhaps it is a wasted effort since every one sooner or later will experience it for himself. But if this journal has a specific message it is an attempt to convey something of the quality of our living, its joy and beauty and fulness of life beyond any human comprehension. It is also a warning that whatever one sows on earth will be fully reaped here.

Hell exists, as it has always done, in the feelings and spirits of men and it can indubitably be brought here with them. Purgation there is, since none of us comes here in perfected form and the wise man will set to work here and now to judge and know himself and to begin to correct those errors, falsenesses and weaknesses which he discovers in his soul. Death will launch him into a world where his emotional being, healthy or diseased, will be the physical equipment with which he starts a new life. We all have to earn our heaven, and every step on the way to the final bliss of pure being is paid for by effort. Yet this record is useless if it has not shown the greatness of the reward and the glory of the whole adventure of living and dying.